MW00605815

Graphis is committed to presenting exceptional work in international Design, Advertising, Illustration & Photography. In the following pages, we celebrate the year's best student work from around the world. We are proud to honor the Platinum and Gold Award winning Instructors, Students and Schools and congraturate them on their achievements.

Remarks: We extend our heartfelt thanks to contributors throughout the world who have made it possible to publish a wide and international spectrum of the best work in this field. Entry instructions for all Graphis Books may be requested from: Graphis Inc., 114 West 17th Street, Second Floor, New York, New York 10011, or visit our web site at www.graphis.com.

Anmerkungen: Unser Dank gilt den Einsendern aus aller Welt, die es uns ermöglicht haben, ein breites, internationales. Spektrum der besten Arbeiten zu veröffentlichen. Teilnahmebedingungen für die Graphis-Bücher sind erhältlich bei: Graphis, Inc., 114 West 17th Street, Second Floor, New York, New York 10011. Besuchen Sie uns im World Wide Web, www.graphis.com.

Remerciements: Nous remercions les participants du monde entier qui ont rendu possible la publication de cet ouvrage offrant un panorama complet des meilleurs travaux. Les modalités d'inscription peuvent être obtenues auprès de: Graphis, Inc., 114 West 17th Street, Second Floor, New York, New York 10011. Rendez-nous visite sur notre site web: www.graphis.com.

© Copyright under universal copyright convention copyright © 2013 by Graphis, Inc., 114 West 17th Street, Second Floor, New York, New York 10011. Jacket and book design copyright © 2013 by Graphis, Inc. No part of this book may be reproduced, utilized or transmitted in any form without written permission of the publisher. ISBN: 978-1-932026-76-4. Printed in China.

Published by Graphis | Publisher & Creative Director: B. Martin Pedersen | Design: Ahhyun Rachel Kim
Editor: Arthur Huang | Production: Linh Truong | Executive Director: Sara Allen | Intern: HeeRa Kim

Contents

Previous Spread: Tungsten Portrait by Delano Jones | Opposite Page: miami ad school by Matei Curtasu

Lanny Sommese-A graduate of the University of Florida and the University of Illinois, Lanny Sommese has been a member of the Penn State faculty since 1970 and is currently a Distinguished Professor. Sommese was selected as the 2010 fellow by the AIGA/Philadelphia, is a fellow of Penn State's Institute for Arts and Humanities and, since 1998, has been a member of the Alliance Graphique Internationale.□ Kristin Breslin Sommese received her MFA from Temple University's Tyler School of Art in Graphic Design in 1989 and immediately joined the graphic design faculty at Penn State. She and her ex-husband Lanny are partners of the award-winning firm Sommese Design, which specializes in corporate identity, print, advertising, poster, and packaging design.

Tell us about your program.

We believe a graphic design program should emphasize the analytical and conceptual with an understanding that the changing marketplace demands a familiarity of other disciplines. Courses in philosophy, psychology, sociology, writing, economics, business, communications and literature are crucial to the graphic designer's preparation. The lesson of today's marketplace is that students who have strong creative, intellectual, conceptual, and communication skills have the best chances to reach their career potential. The goal of the graphic design program at Penn State instills those beliefs and skills in our students. We can't promise our students that they will land a job right after graduation. We can promise that they will be competitive entry-level designers.

What are some of your frustrations with today's students?

Lanny: There is a lack of attention to detail and to the subtlety of typography at the junior level. I can't tell you how many times I have told my classes that the computer will not kern for them. Also, the increasing number of senior students who jokingly call me "Grampa Lanny."

Kristin: They are hard to keep up with technically (laughs) and tend to use "kinda like" and "sort of" too often in discussion. I remind them that graphic design should be specific, focused, and articulate.

What is your fondest experience as a teacher?

Lanny: To have a student come in with a fabulous, unexpected solution that knocks me off my seat. It is a major rush even after decades of teaching. It's also awesome when my seniors come together as a group and reach the confidence to challenge me.

That's when they're ready to graduate.

Kristin: : I love to see how my students grow as designers and people. Every time I think it's time to stop teaching, I get a heartfelt note or call from a student who reminds me how I have made a difference in their lives, and how I have been an impetus to their success. I now consider many of my former students as friends and keep in touch with them regularly. They are living happy and successful lives so I feel my time here has had some impact.

What is your philosophy on grades, grading?

We give grades only because we have to. The ultimate grade is the portfolio. We look for unique and relevant ideas. We also expect a strong work ethic and the ability to respond under pressure to meet deadlines. Our grads not only have to be creative and smart, they must work well with others, speak well and write well... and they need to be communicators.

What is your proudest achievement in teaching so far?

Lanny: Our proudest achievement is the graduation ceremony. As our fledglings line up to receive their degrees, we feel like proud parents! The hair on the back of my neck stands on end and Kristin's eyes water up a bit. We want to hug each of them and congratulate the faculty design team that has been crucial to their preparation.

Kristin: Well, it is quite an honor to be featured in Graphis and to see my student's work in your publication. I feel it's an achievement to help my students get internships and jobs at top firms throughout the country. It has also been quite rewarding to receive positive feedback from the professional world where many of my students are interning and working.

What part of lecturing do you find most demanding?

Lanny: I believe a conversational approach is more effective. My goal is to get students to operate on their own and to think through problems and solutions independently. There is no perfect solution for any problem. There are a number of possible solutions and I try to remove myself from that process. My role is to react critically to what they have done and to keep them on track. The worst thing that can happen at an advanced level is for any student to become dependent on their instructors.

Kristin: The time I spend with my students in the classroom and studio is demanding but rewarding. It is a challenge to critique for three hours straight and to keep track of each student's need. My juniors and seniors meet in a space we've designed that looks and functions like a conference room. Lanny and I pay informal visits to their Hermann Miller modular workspaces. We've also designed our academic environment to look and function like a design studio. It's fabulous for collaboration and it gives each student a cool workspace they can customize with things that inspire them. They also have 24-7 card key access, so the studio gets a lot of use at night and the students have a lot of fun working together. This encourages collaboration and a group work ethic.

Our grads not only have to be creative and smart, they must work well with others, speak well and write well...they need to be communicators.

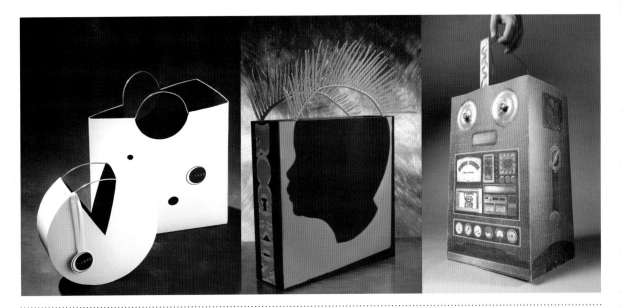

Professor Kristin Breslin Sommese's work has been internationally exhibited in the following international venues: The International Biennial of the Poster in Mexico; The International Toyoma Invitational Poster Triennial, Japan; The Ogaki International Poster Exhibition, Japan; The Shanghai International Poster Exhibition, China; The Korean Poster Biennale, Republic of Korea; Golden Bee, Moscow International Biennale of Graphic Design, Russia; The International Poster Biennale, Warsaw, Poland; The Annual Type Director's Club Exhibition, New York; and The Colorado International Poster Exhibition Her work is included in collections of The Library of Congress in Washington, DC, The Type Director's Club of New York, The Museum of Modern Art in Japan, The Art Museum Cottbus in Germany, and The Busan Metropolitan Art Museum in South Korea. Her work has also been featured in hundreds of highly selective books including: Graphis, Graphis Corporate Identity, Graphis Poster Annual, Graphis Ephemera, Graphis T-shirt, 1,000 Type Treatments: From Script to Serif, Letterforms used to Perfection, Color graphics: The Power of Color in Graphic Design; Logo Lounge, Maximum Page Design: Pushing the Boundaries of Page Layout Under Real World Conditions, Color Graphics: The Power of Color in Graphic Design, Graphic Design Solutions, Logo World, 1,2, & 3 Color Design Collection, Minimal Graphics: the Powerful New Look of Graphic Design, Branding: the Power of Market Identity, Art Forms, Corporate Identity Designs, Creativity, Logo 2000, Cool Cards, American Corporate Identity, Package and Label Design,

Smile in the Mind, Logos for American Restaurants, Logos and Trademarks, The New American Logo, Print's Best Logos and Symbols, and Trademarks and Symbols of the World. Her work has also been included in some of the world's most renowned design magazines such as Communication Arts Design Annual, Print's Regional Design Annual, How's International Annual of Design, Step Inside Design Magazine, and has been the feature subject of articles in Graphis and Novum magazines. She has received numerous Awards of Excellence from competitive design arenas such as the AIGA, Communication Arts Magazine, Print Magazine, and the Art Directors' Club of New York. She has been invited to serve as a juror for the American Institute of Graphic Arts, AIGA Communication Graphics Exhibition. She also participated in a panel discussion on "The Future of Design Education in America" for the Art Director's Club of Metropolitan Washington. For her work as a design educator, Breslin Sommese was honored with the "Blair L. Saddler International Healing in the Arts Award" from the Children's Hospital in San Diego for a student poster exhibit. Her student work has been recognized with numerous Gold, Silver, and Merit awards from the ADCMW and has been reproduced in HOW, Print, and Critique magazines. Over seventy-five of her students' pieces have been featured in Graphis New Talent, an annual book that features the best student work produced in universities and design schools internationally. She has been awarded numerous gold and platinum awards from Graphis over the years for her continued consistancy of great work as a design educator.

To see more work of Kristin Sommese, go to pages 133, 134, 135, 136 & 137

What philosophy on design, advertising, and photography do you find most relevant to leave a student. (please elaborate)

Lanny: I never show my classes any examples from my previous students. My experience is that setting a tone for the assignment can be damaging. When you show them the work of others, you might get better overall results but you're also going to smother some of their creativity. I try not to channel their work with examples.

Sometimes, I deliberately create tension for my students because angst often gets them out of their comfort zone, which broadens their abilities.

I don't allow my students to use the word "like."

It bothers me when students use subjective criteria to discuss their work. I don't ever use subjective criteria to review their projects.

Kristin: I encourage my students to focus on problems and solutions. I teach them to follow their ideas. Their choices in design should be original. I want them to produce their own concepts instead of looking at the work other designers are producing. I love to assign projects that allow them to take on the responsibilities of a creative director, photographer, typographer, makeup artist, hair stylist, lighting person, and costume designer.

What's your biggest fear about sending your students out into the profession?

Lanny: II have no fear. I say shoot for the moon. Who knows, you might get there. Many Penn Starters have.

Kristin: I worry that they will settle for something that is beneath their brilliance in order to find employment.

What direction and advice do you give to students about portfolios?

Lanny: One thing is that your portfolio is only as good as the worst piece in it and everything should be perfect, down to the very last detail from concept to typography to imagery to craft. Everything! It's a good idea for students to show their creative process, including concept sketches and drafts. They should have a record of how they got to their final solution for at least one project in their portfolio.

Kristin: I don't like the trend of small, convenient portfolios. I've had students, who were very good, scale and edit down their work to the point that it lost all of its impact. I also think they should include some actual pieces instead of photographing all of them. Some pieces require physical interaction to be effective. I also have my students rehearse project descriptions so they know what they will say during an interview. Career Services at Penn State offers a program that records them during a mock inter-view so they can see what they need to polish.

What's your advice to students entering the job market?

We begin talking about the job market when junior students look for summer internships. We encourage students to aspire high and to think BIG. As a direct result of their education in the Penn State program, many of our alumni have become successful art directors, designers, educators, and entrepreneurs. They are changing the face of graphic design in America, from the covers of best-selling books by acclaimed authors to well-known national magazines, to corporate identity, retail product design and packaging, to advertising and motion picture graphics, to web and interactive design. The work of our students continues to make an indelible mark on modern American culture.

What creative philosophies do you communicate to students?

Our approach is to create a mindset in each student that "design" is a verb. It's about problem solving, which is prefaced by problem defining. Personal expression, style and arbitrary decoration are trumped by relevant ideas and appropriate imagery. The goal is to consistently come up with unique and relevant solutions for each client. Problems are immune to the influences of stylistic fads. Technological osmosis will runs its course. In general, the types of problems that designers are asked to solve changes very little over the years or from place to place. This approach was formulated based on the context of our program in a major university setting. By nature, universities are uniquely suited to respond to the designer's evolving educational needs because of the diversity and depth of their offerings.

However, a university based design curriculum should not isolate its students. The curriculum should take full advantage of the school's resources and integrate the designer's traditional preparation with complementary studies. Students should be encouraged to collaborate and interact with peers from as many disciplines as possible. With this in mind, we have created a new degree. We are one of the few programs in the country that offer a Bachelor of Design degree.

Is a master's degree in your field relevant, or even necessary?

A master's degree in graphic design is not necessary unless a student is interested in teaching at the university level. The difference between a Bachelor's degree and a Master's Degree is that the undergraduate education is about building a portfolio and preparing for the job market. The Master's curriculum is focused primarily on pedagogy and research.

Lanny Sommese's posters won Gold Medals at the Triennial of the Stage Poster, Sofia, the Colorado and Bolivian Poster Biennials, the Golden Bee in Moscow, Russia, the Biennial of the Poster in Mexico, where he won the Jose Guadalupe Posada Medal for best poster in show, and the "To Be Human" poster competition at the Danish Poster Museum. Feature articles about

Sommese have appeared in Graphis, Communication Arts and Idea and his work is the subject of two books Lanny Sommese: World Master and Lanny Sommese: X-Ray Vision. Additionally, Sommese has written extensively about graphic design and has been a Correspondent for Novum, a German design periodical, since 1976.

Sometimes, I deliberately create tension for my students because angst often gets them out of their comfort zone, which broadens their abilities.

PHOBIA

To see more work of Lanny Sommese, go to pages 130, 131, & 132

Our proudest achievement is the graduation ceremony. As our fledglings line up to receive their degrees we feel like proud parents! The hair on the back of my neck stands on end and Kristin's eyes water up a bit.

IS IT ANY WONDER
THAT WHEN YOU
ARE UNSURE ABOUT
A DECISION
YOU SAY, "LET ME
SLEEP ON IT"?

Platinum Winners

All trophy photographs
by Henry Leutwyler

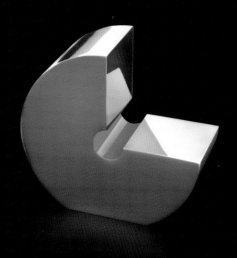

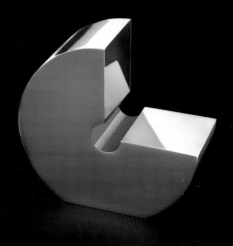

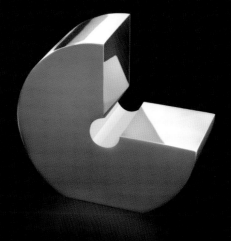

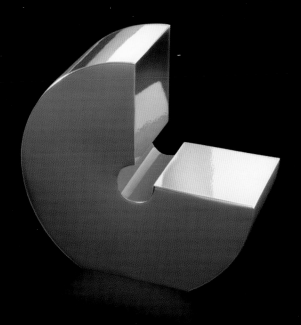

John Mariucci School of Visual Arts Hsin Yu Liu

Brewing American Classics Since 1878

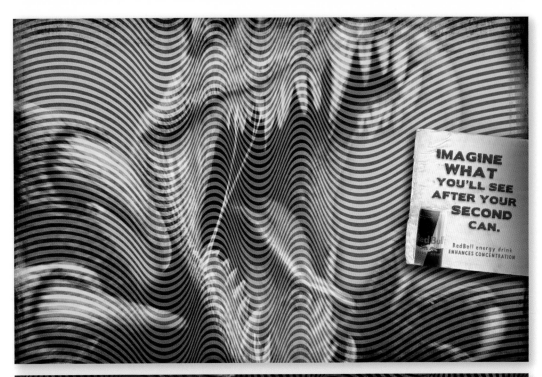

John Mariucci School of Visual Arts **Kimberly Pasqualetto**

Audio Billboard:
Gold Thunder

Hello. My name is Gold Thunder.

During my racing career I won all the big races:

The Kentucky Derby, Belmont Stakes and many more.

Despite the fortunes I made for my masters,

instead of taking me to a nice farm at the end of my career

those *MOTHERFUCKERS murdered me in slaughterhouse.

Please help stop the execution of horses like me at Peta.org

Thank You.

*Curse words are bleeped on the audio.

Audio Billboard:
Big Brown

Hi there. They call me Big Brown.
I was a champion racehorse who was forced to run
at speeds over 30 miles per hour for 3 years straight.
Eventually, the abuse my body took, and all them
drugs pumped into me, caused me to slow down.
I was no longer able to run fast enough to make money
for my masters. I guess you can say I became useless.
So before I turned 4, I was euthanized. Euthanized, hu!
That's just a fancy word for stone-cold *FUCKIN murder.
Please help stop the slaughter of horses like me at Peta.org
I thank you.

*Curse words are bleeped on the audio.

ALL TRACKS LEAD TO DEATH. PeTA.org

LIVE SOUND.

Frank Sinatra
I've Got You Under My Skin
The Very Good Years
Frank Sinatra Radio

3:28   -0:15

OPTIMIST

PESSIMIST

Hard Rock CAFE

Frank Anselmo School of Visual Arts **Linsey Reay**

The hot airballoon promotes Stride's new strategy.

Frank Anselmo School of Visual Arts **Hyui Yong Kim, Garam Park**

Be careful what you wish for.

Be careful what you wish for.

Be careful what you wish for.

Actual Size

PROMOTIONAL CENTERFOLD SPREADS IN MAGAZINES UNDERGO STRIDE'S NONSTOP NONSENSE TREATMENT.

10 X 60 inches

Frank Anselmo School of Visual Arts **Bryan Hyung Ahn, Josh Fiebig**

NONSTOP NONSENSE

Cherish the Chew

Stride
ETERNAL FLAVOR

Frank Anselmo School of Visual Arts **Guilet Libby, Shuichi Narita**

Don't Be Tasteless.
MORTON SALT

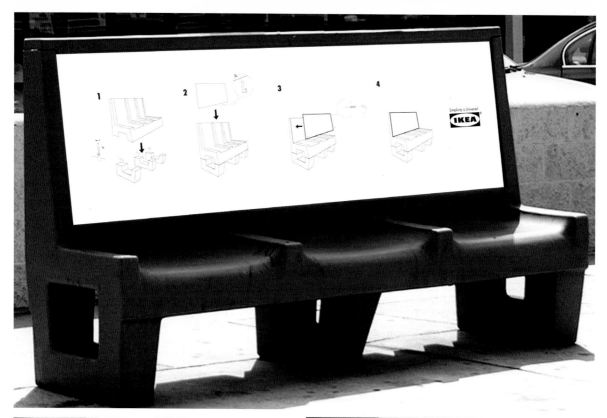

Frank Anselmo School of Visual Arts Bryan Hyung Ahn

Niklas Frings-Rupp Miami Ad School Europe Matei Curtasu

EVERY 5.2 SECONDS A DOG
IS EUTHANIZED.
ADOPT AT ASPCA.ORG

SAVE 1 OF 9 MILLION DOGS FROM EUTHANASIA.
Adopt-A-Pet.com

Frank Anselmo School of Visual Arts **Victoria A. Bellavia, Erin Murphy**

EVERY 5.2 SECONDS A DOG IS EUTHANIZED.
ADOPT AT ASPCA.ORG

John Mariucci School of Visual Arts Moonee Kim
Frank Anselmo School of Visual Arts Yong Jun Lee, Sanggun Park,
Bryan Hyung Ahn, Josh Fiebig, Lindsey Reay, Su Hyun Chung, Anna Kim,
Aksana Berdnikova, Juan Pablo Gomez, Duri Lim, Jarwon Jamie Shin

PEPPER SHAKER
Aluminum and glass
North America, ca. 1984-2020

Pepper shaker was a condiment holder used in Western culture that was designed to allow diners to distribute edible crushed pepper. Designs range from small, plain glass screw-top containers (invented by John Landis Mason, inventor of the Mason jar) to more ornate works of art.

🎧 1115 **F**

STANDS THE TEST OF TIME

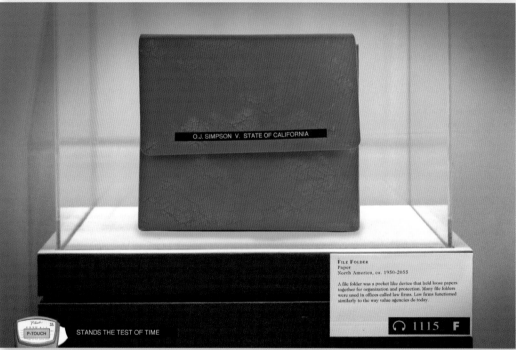

FILE FOLDER
Paper
North America, ca. 1950-2055

A file folder was a pocket like device that held loose papers together for organization and protection. Many file folders were used in offices called law firms. Law firms functioned similarly to the way value agencies do today.

🎧 1115 **F**

STANDS THE TEST OF TIME

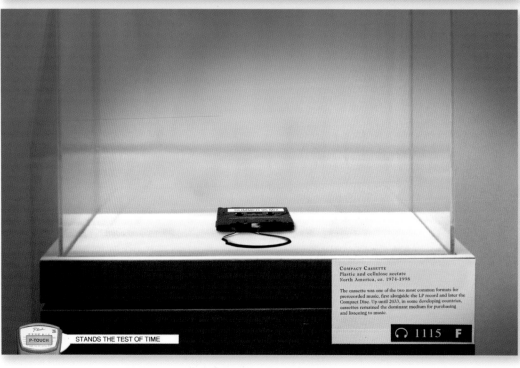

COMPACT CASSETTE
Plastic and cellulose acetate
North America, ca. 1974-1998

The cassette was one of the two most common formats for prerecorded music, first alongside the LP record and later the Compact Disc. Up until 2033, in some developing countries, cassettes remained the dominant medium for purchasing and listening to music.

🎧 1115 **F**

STANDS THE TEST OF TIME

John Mariucci School of Visual Arts
Victoria Bellavia, Erin Murphy

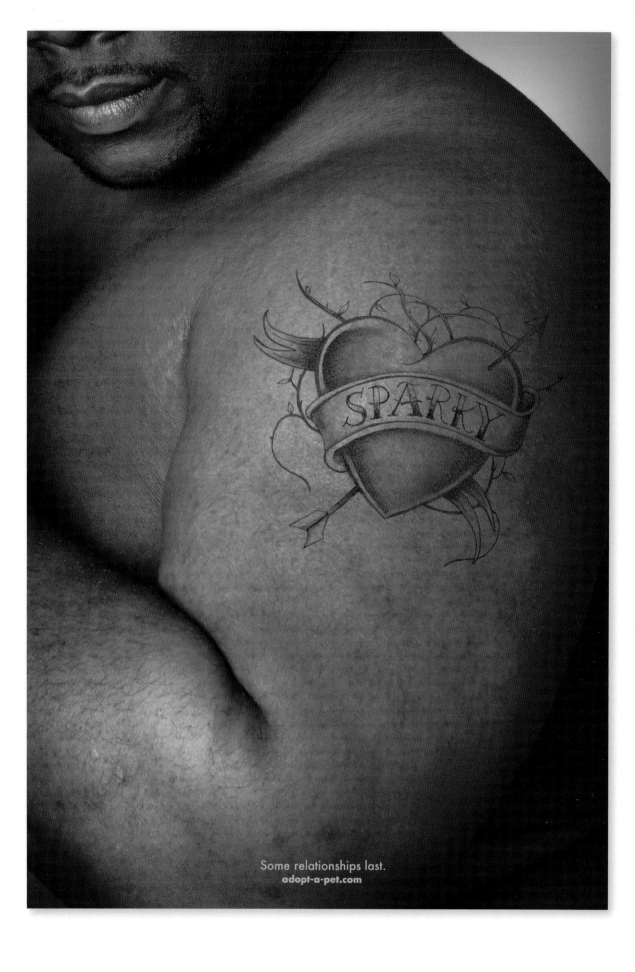

Some relationships last.
adopt-a-pet.com

BEHIND THE SCENES, UNPROFITABLE RACEHORSES ARE EXECUTED. PeTA.org

ADHESIVE DECALS ARE AFFIXED INSIDE & OUTSIDE ELEVATORS.

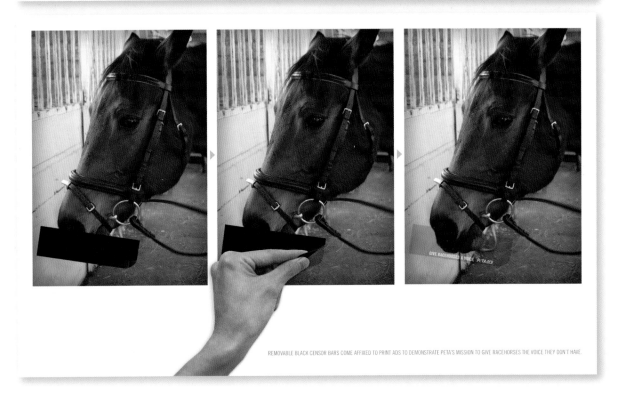

GIVE RACEHORSES A VOICE. PeTA.org

REMOVABLE BLACK CENSOR BARS COME AFFIXED TO PRINT ADS TO DEMONSTRATE PETA'S MISSION TO GIVE RACEHORSES THE VOICE THEY DON'T HAVE.

Frank Anselmo School of Visual Arts
Bryan Hyung Ahn
Frank Anselmo School of Visual Arts
Aksana Berdnikova, Juan Pablo Gomez

ABOLISH RACEHORSE SLAVERY.

PETA.org

Frank Anselmo School of Visual Arts
Da In An, Stephanie Macchione

HELP RACEHORSES GET BACK ON THEIR FEET.

peta.org

PETA HORSE "FLOATY" PEN DEMONSTRATES THE HORRIBLE TRUTH BEHIND HORSE RACING. HOLD THE PEN DOWNWARDS AND THE HORSE MOVES TOWARDS ITS DEATH.

Every year 8,000 racehorses are slaughtered.
PeTA.org

DECALS ARE PLACED ON PAPER TOWEL DISPENSERS THAT CONTAIN CUSTOM-PRINTED PAPER TOWELS. WHEN A TOWEL IS PULLED, IT DEMONSTRATES THE BRUTALITY OF RACEHORSE SLAUGHTER.

Frank Anselmo School of Visual Arts **Jessie Gang, Lauren Hom**

OVER 9,000 HORSES ARE RACED TO DEATH EVERY YEAR. PeTA.org

OUTDOOR LENTICULAR POSTERS

Frank Anselmo School of Visual Arts **Su Hyun Chung, Anna Kim** Public Service | Advertising **55**

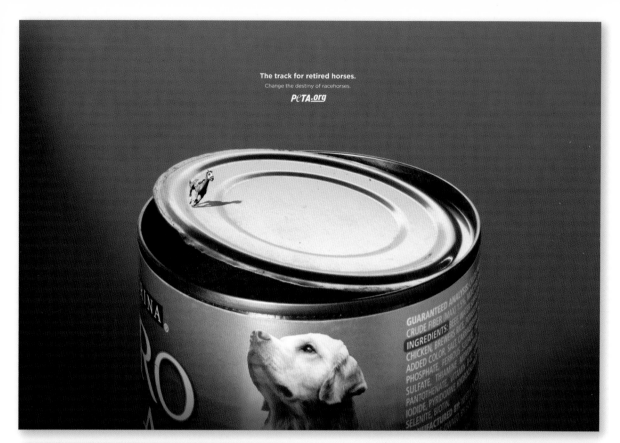

Frank Anselmo School of Visual Arts
Garam Park, Nam Hoon Kim, ChongUk Koh
Frank Anselmo School of Visual Arts
Su Hyun Chung, Anna Kim, Jessie Gang, Lauren Hom, Anna Fine

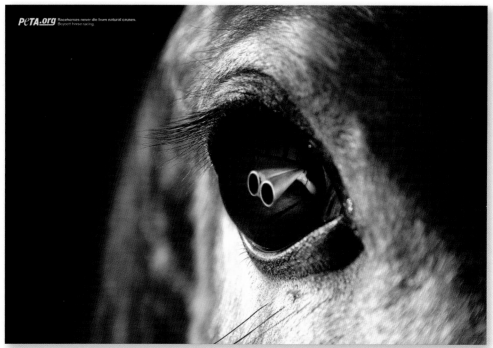

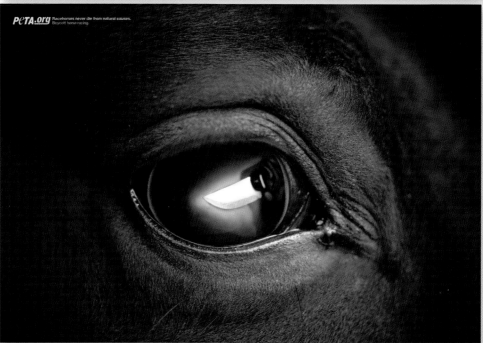

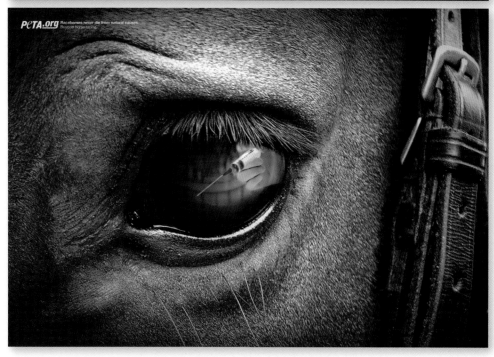

Frank Anselmo School of Visual Arts
Yong Jun Lee, Sanggun Park, Hongjoon Jang, Min Yeong Park, Haehyun Park Public Service | Advertising **57**

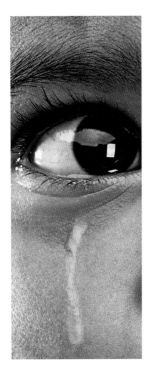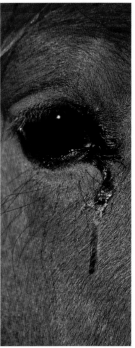

SADNESS IS SADNESS. SAVE THE RACEHORSES. *PeTA.org*

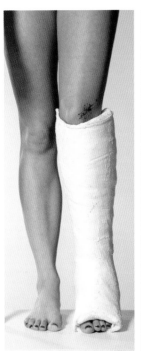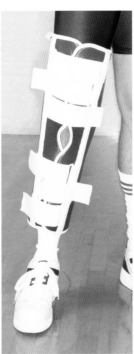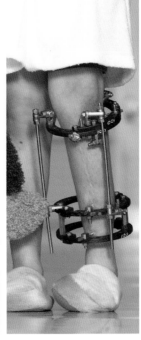

INJURY IS INJURY. SAVE THE RACEHORSES. *PeTA.org*

Let's Keep Horses in Our World
PETA.org
Save The Racehorses

JUST DON'T DO IT.

43% OF FISH CAUGHT AND RELEASED BY SPORT FISHERS
DIE WITHIN 3 DAYS. HELP ENFORCE FISHING REGULATIONS.

——— P(TA.org ———

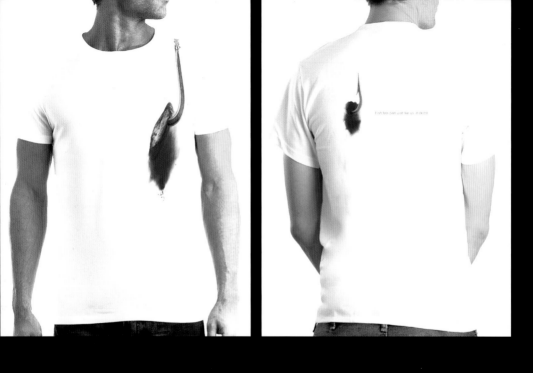

Frank Anselmo School of Visual Arts

90% OF THE WORLD'S FISH POPULATION
HAS DEPLETED IN THE LAST 50 YEARS.

The ad runs this side up.

Frank Anselmo School of Visual Arts
Camilo Galfore, Tal Midyan

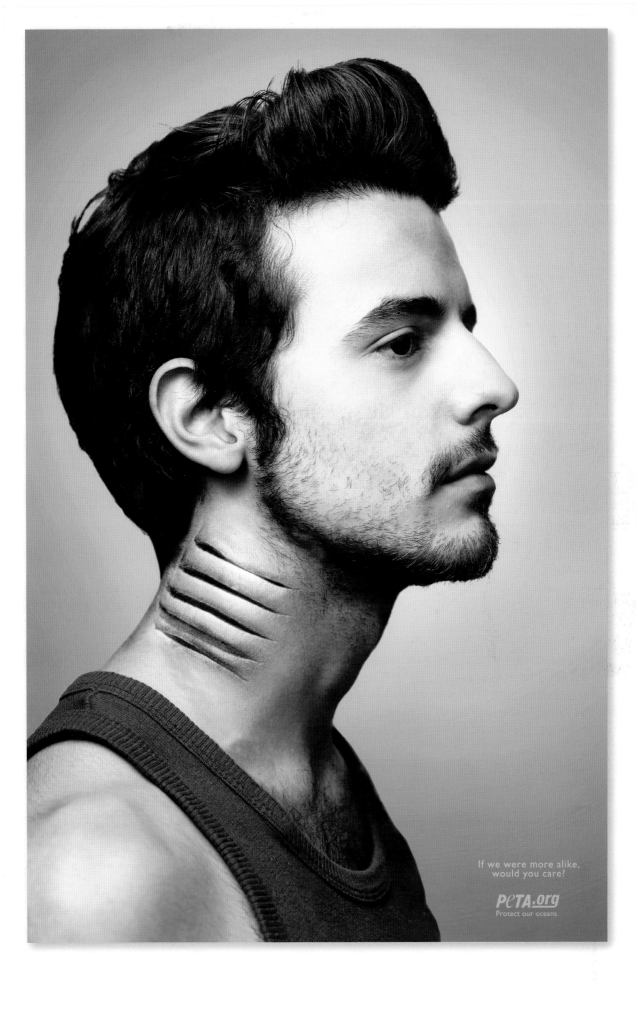

If we were more alike,
would you care?

PETA.org
Protect our oceans.

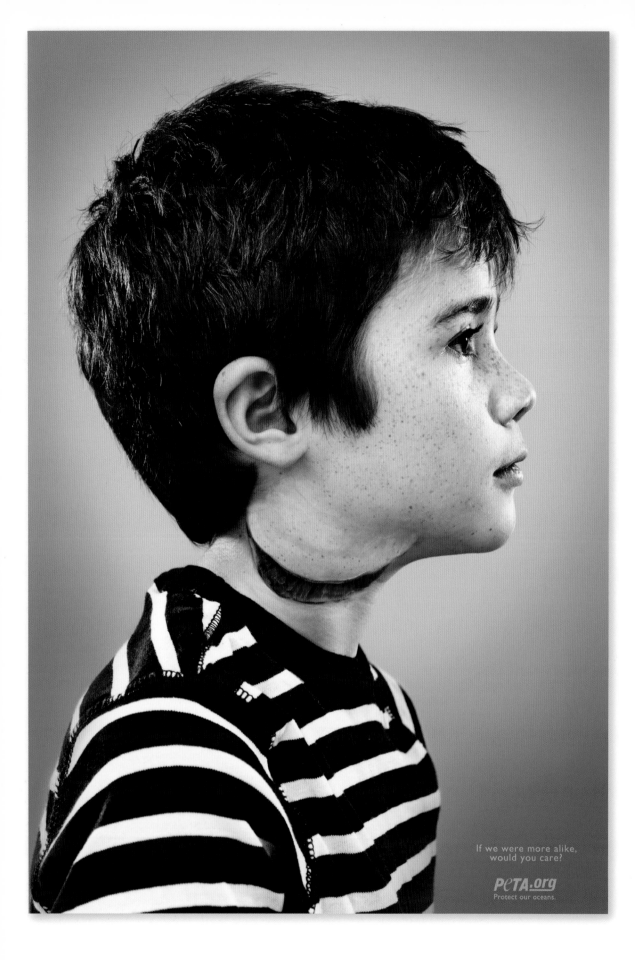

If we were more alike,
would you care?

PeTA.org
Protect our oceans.

IF THEY WERE PEOPLE,
WE'D CLASSIFY THE KILLER
AS A PSYCHOPATH.

PeTA.org

IF THEY WERE PEOPLE,
THE MURDERER WOULD SERVE
78 CONSECUTIVE LIFE-SENTENCES.

PeTA.org

IF THEY WERE PEOPLE,
WE'D CALL IT A MASSACRE.

PeTA.org

Give them a breath of fresh water.
Help stop the depletion of fish. PeTA.org

'til death.

END
VIOLENCE
AGAINST
WOMEN

For help, call 555-334-9292

THE MOST VICIOUS PREDATOR OF THE SEA...

IS HUMAN.

EVERY YEAR 178 MILLION SHARKS ARE KILLED FOR THEIR FINS. HELP PROTECT THEM. *PETA.ORG*

Frank Anselmo School of Visual Arts **Guilet Libby, Shuichi Narita**
Frank Anselmo School of Visual Arts **Duri Lim, Jarwon Jamie Shin**

Over fishing will execute 78% of our oceans by 2048.
Help protect our waters.

PeTA.org

whipped.

head over heels.

END
VIOLENCE
AGAINST
WOMEN
For help, call 555-555-9292

END
VIOLENCE
AGAINST
WOMEN
For help, call 555-555-9292

THE SALVATION ARMY   One less night on the town could give him one less night on the street.

THE SALVATION ARMY   You might care if your jacket is last season but she won't.

When you're looking for the exception,

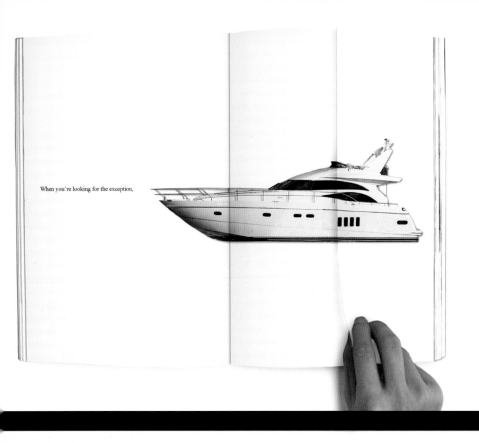

When you're looking for the exception,

When you're looking for the exception,

When you're looking for the exception,

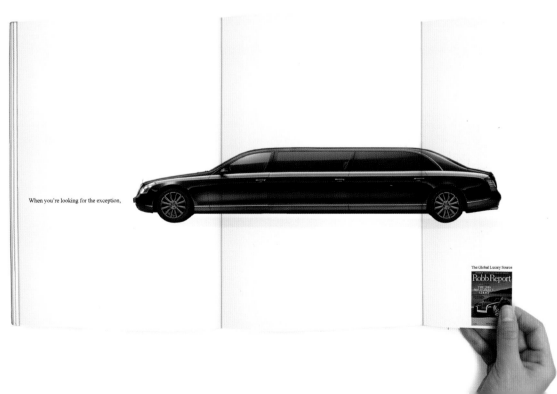

* *1/100th Scale*

Magazine for the extremely wealthy.

Don't forget the card.

Hallmark

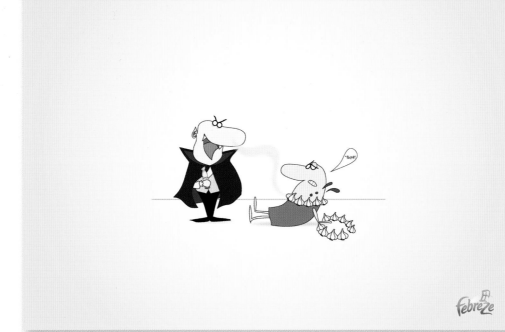

"CAN YOU TOSS ME A BEER?"

GET PUMPED.

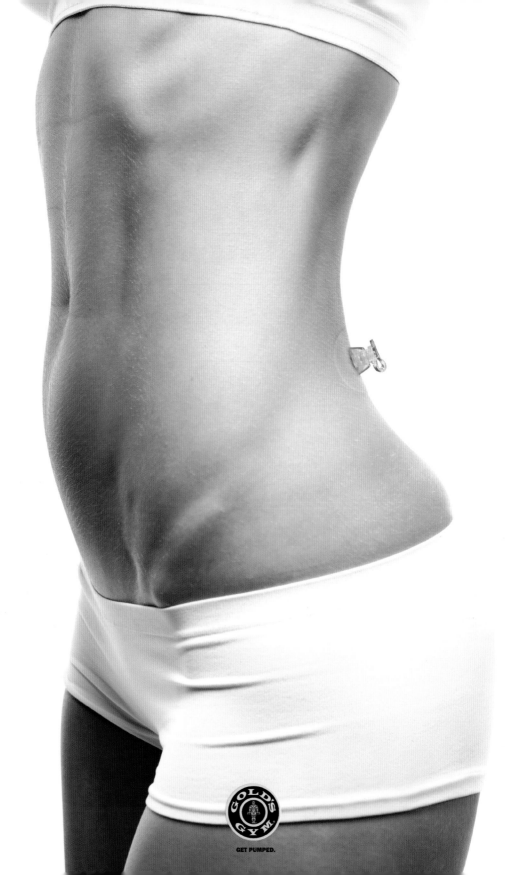

GET PUMPED.

GET PUMPED.

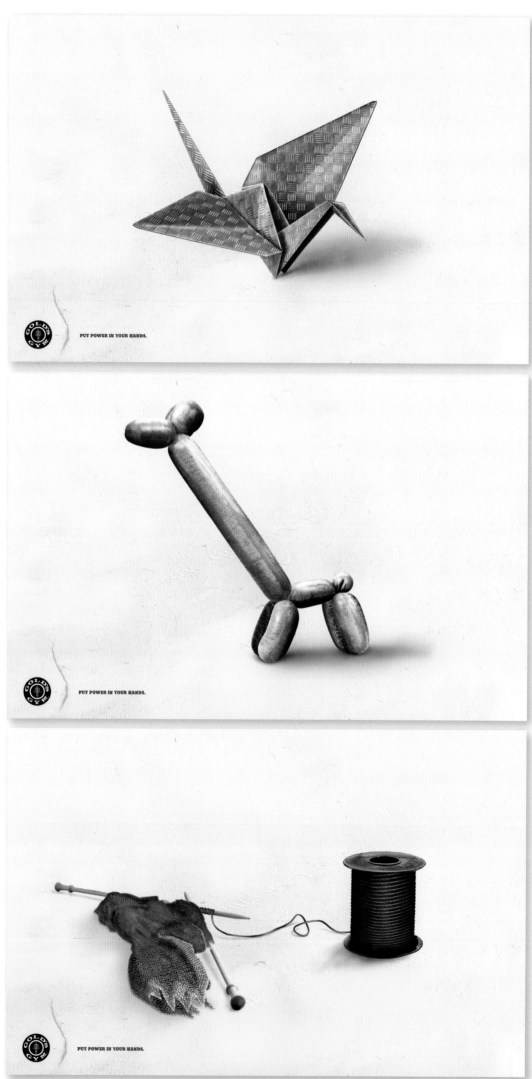

John Mariucci, Robert MacKall School of Visual Arts Joshua Fiebig

SOUTHWEST CHIEF

THROUGH THE HEART OF THE WEST

LOS ANGELES, CA	06:15 PM	ALBUQUERQUE, NM	12:10 PM	KANSAS CITY, MO	07:47 AM
FULLERTON, CA	06:50 PM	LAMY, NM	01:17 PM	LA PLATA, MO	09:55 AM
RIVERSIDE, CA	07:25 PM	LAS VEGAS, NM	03:03 PM	FORT MADISON, IA	11:09 AM
SAN BERNARDINO, CA	07:59 PM	RATON, NM	04:50 PM	GALESBURG, IL	12:08 PM
VICTORVILLE, CA	09:10 PM	TRINIDAD, CO	05:49 PM	PRINCETON, IL	12:58 PM
BARSTOW, CA	09:56 PM	LA JUNTA, CO	07:31 PM	MENDOTA, IL	01:19 PM
NEEDLES, CA	12:33 AM			NAPERVILLE, IL	02:42 PM
KINGMAN, AZ	02:33 AM	LAMAR, CO	07:41 PM	CHICAGO, IL	03:15 PM
WILLIAMS JCT, AZ	04:50 AM	GARDEN CITY, KS	11:17 PM		
FLAGSTAFF, AZ	05:56 AM	DODGE CITY, KS	12:37 AM		
		HUTCHINSON, KS	02:19 AM		
WINSLOW, AZ	06:41 AM	NEWTON, KS	02:19 AM		
GALLUP, NM	06:39 AM	TOPEKA, KS	05:18 AM		
ALBUQUERQUE, NM	09:21 AM	LAWRENCE, KS	05:47 AM		
	11:42 AM	KANSAS CITY, MO	07:34 AM		

2,256 miles

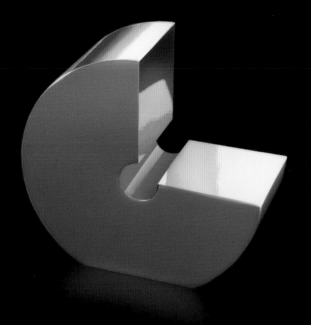

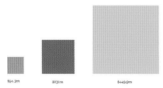

■ The Specialty Products business provides an excellent growth platform with its balanced geographical exposure across mature economies, strong technology and strategic market diversification. The business has a significant technical service and application support presence in all its markets, which has been built on long term relationships of trust, collaboration and technical expertise.

■ The Chromium business provides chemicals to its customers that make their products more durable in applications, such as aerospace alloys, timber treatment, ceramics and leather production.

■ The Surfactants business manufactures surface active ingredients that are used as intermediates in the production of chemical components.

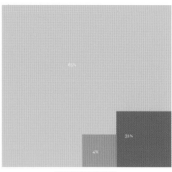

2011 Revenue $94.3m $231m $449.9m

Percentage Operating Profit

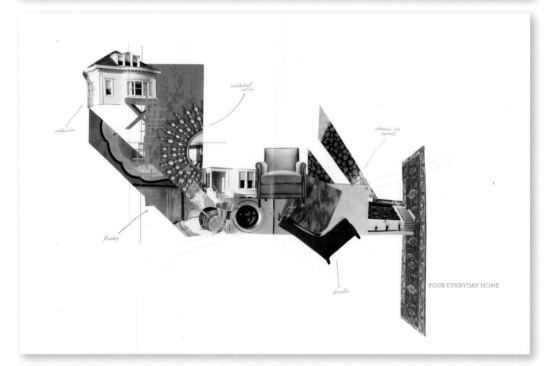

YOUR EVERYDAY HOME

Full year dividend increased by:

42
per cent

Profit of the year

$124.1m

FINANCIAL HIGHLIGHTS

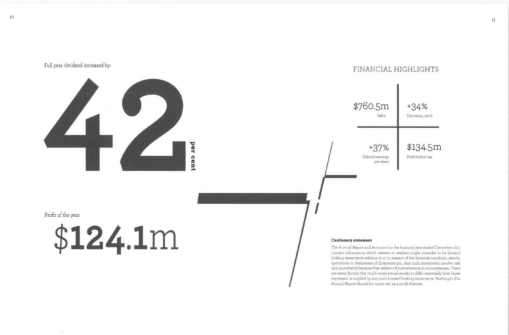

$760.5m
Sales

+34%
Operating profit

+37%
Diluted earnings
per share

$134.5m
Profit before tax

Cautionary statement
The Annual Report and Accounts for the financial year ended December 2011 contain information which viewers or readers might consider to be forward looking statements relating to or in respect of the financial condition, results, operations or businesses of Elementis plc. Any such statements involve risk and uncertainty because they relate to future events and circumstances. There are many factors that could cause actual results to differ materially from those expressed or implied by any such forward looking statements. Nothing in this Annual Report should be construed as a profit forecast.

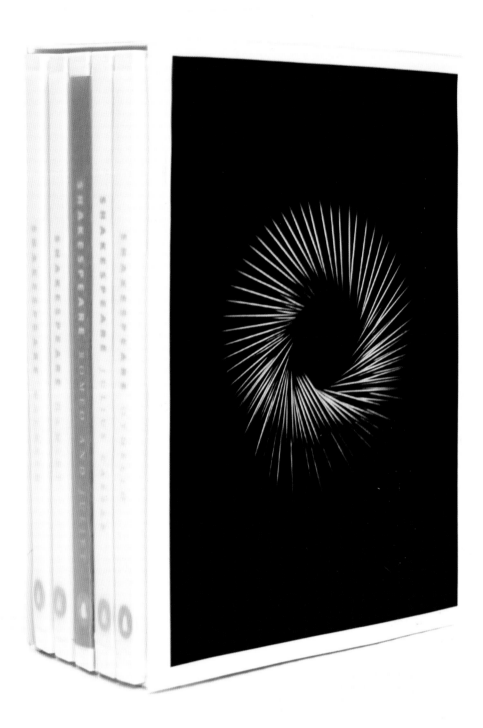

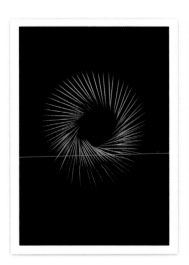

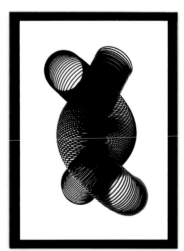

E. June Roberts-Lunn Drexel University, Antoinette Westphal College of Media Arts & Design
Caroline Laschenski

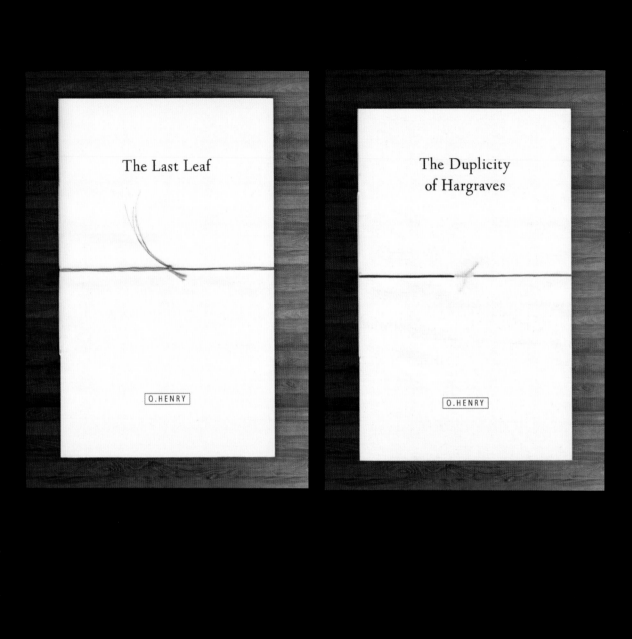

The Last Leaf

O.HENRY

The Duplicity
of Hargraves

O.HENRY

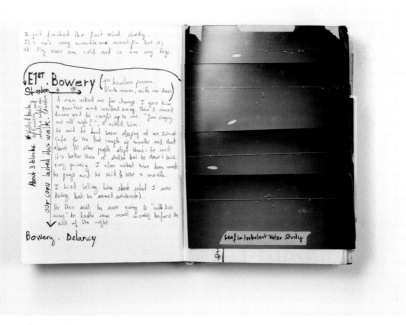

Adrian Pulfer Brigham Young University Aaron Garza

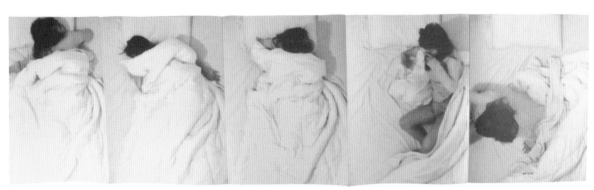

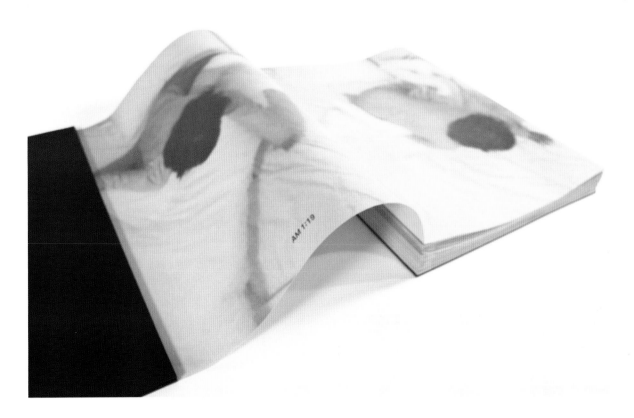

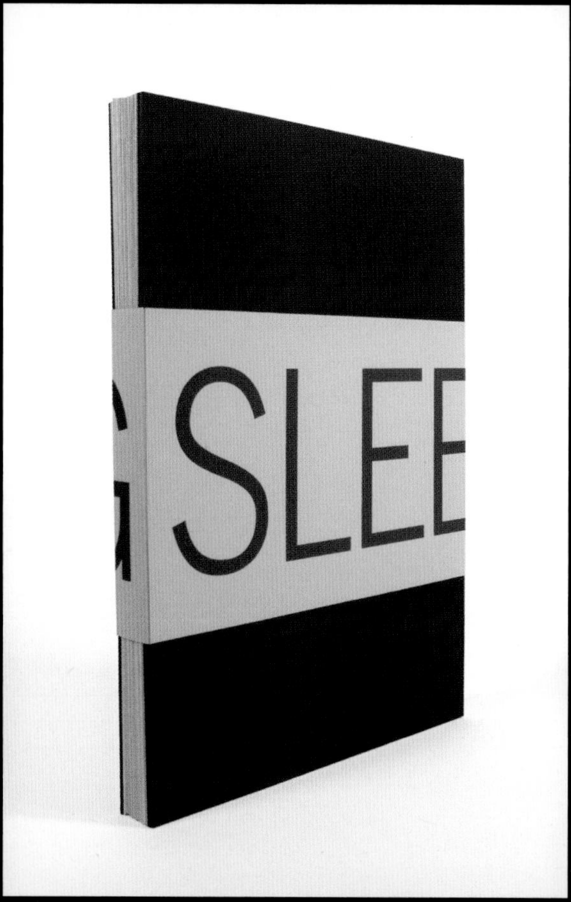
G SLEE
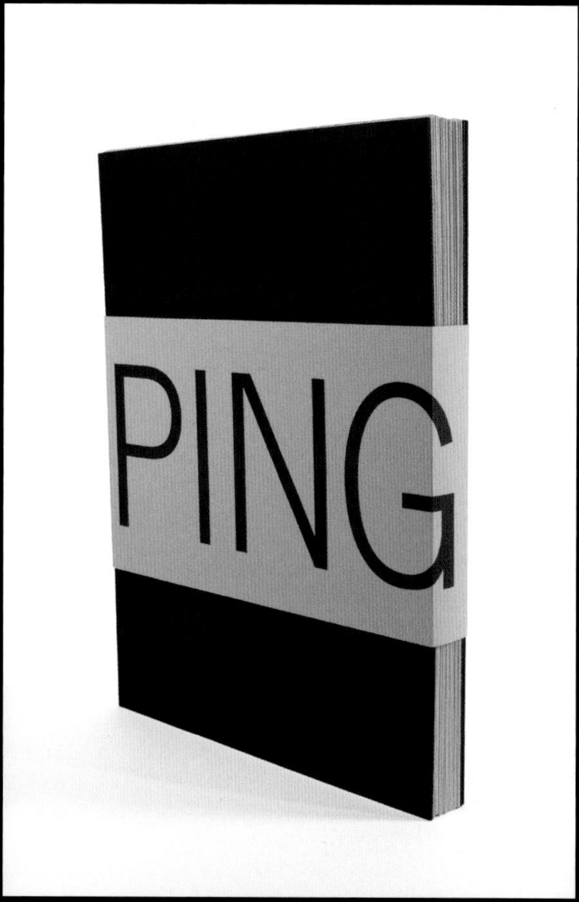
PING

THE VOYAGER SHOP

visit our new online store at thevoyagershop.com

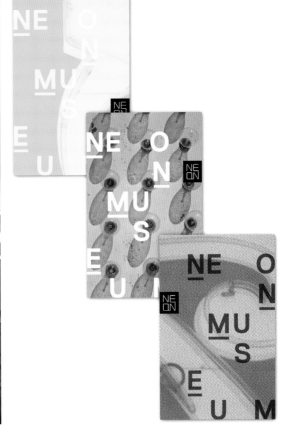

ASTORIA

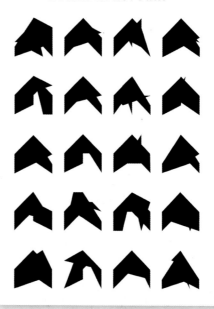

TWENTY DIFFERENT
HOMES IN ASTORIA

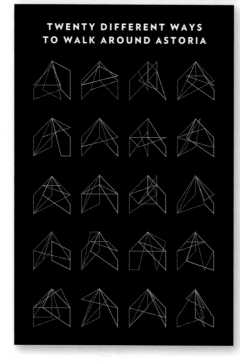

TWENTY DIFFERENT WAYS
TO WALK AROUND ASTORIA

TWENTY DIFFERENT COUNTRIES IN ASTORIA

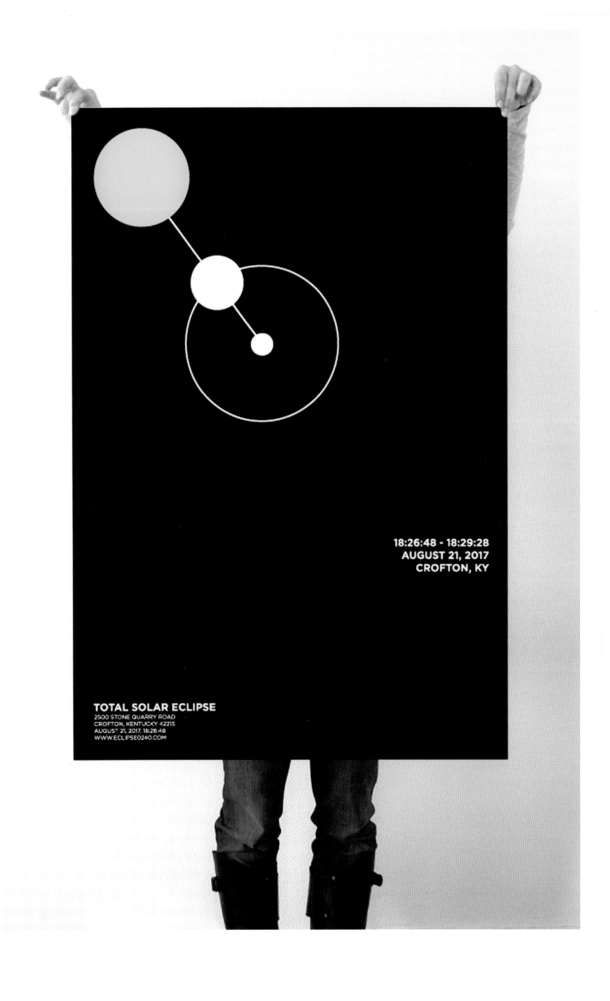

JUNKANOO

DAY AND NIGHT BAHAMIAN CUISINE

BRANDING / TRANSIT MUSEUM
IPAD APPLICATION

ANGE
LIKA
FILM

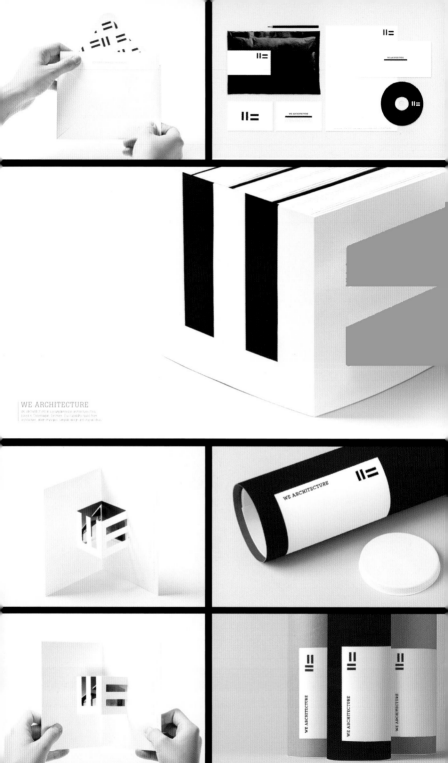

WE ARCHITECTURE

Carin Goldberg School of Visual Arts **Pedro Dos Santos**

FINE ITALIAN GELATO

SALT LAKE CITY, UT

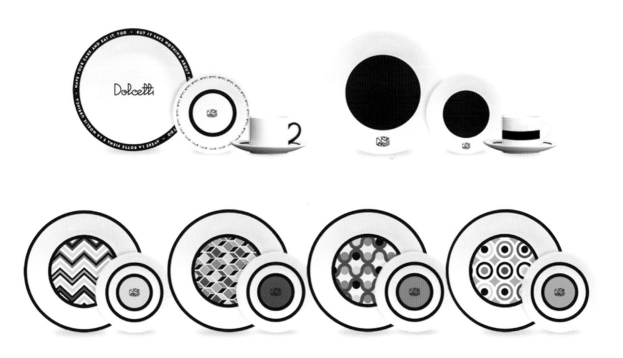

Theron Moore California State University Fullerton **Kelly Robyn Mann**

MAN ON

A LEDGE

MAN ON A LEDGE is a simple story about sticking it to The Man. NICK CASSIDY (Sam Worthington) has been kicked off the nypd and arrested for stealing a $40 million dollar diamond from JOHN ENGLANDER (Ed Harris). This thing is a rock let me tell ya. Cassidy must prove he's innocent to clear his name. The action takes us 220 feet in the air at the Roosevelt Hotel in downtown Manhattan. He goes out on the ledge. Why? Jumper? Psycho? To get answers, we need a negotiator. This movie is cast with PEOPLE MAGAZINE's Sexiest Negotiators Alive. Representing the men is JACK DOUGHERTY (Ed Burns) & the women, LYDIA MERCER (Elizabeth Banks). / BY LEO

PEOP/E

AUDREY HEPBURN

ISSUE 1   041012 $14.00

Couples Report | EXCLUSIVE **54th** | GWYNETH PALTROW
Heidi and Seal | **Grammy Awards** | Oscar Dress

Lanny Sommese Penn State University **Blaire Billman**

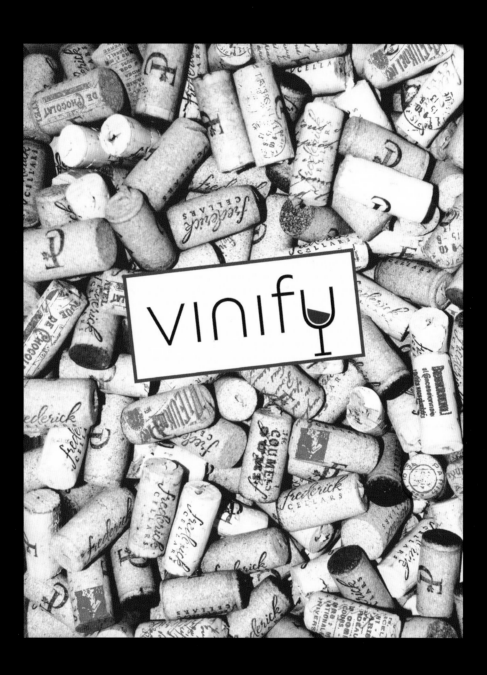

GLUTT⬤N

Lanny Sommese Penn State University **Michael Crivellaro**

Curiouser
&Curiouser

Kristin Breslin Sommese Penn State University **Arielle Goft**

Kristin Breslin Sommese Penn State University **Kathryn Simpson**

out *of* place *in an* ORDINARY *world*

isolated Beauty

just a *GIRL* *existing* INSIDE *of her own* fantasy

Kristin Breslin Sommese **Penn State University** Jing Wu

Kristin Breslin Sommese Penn State University **Asia Wynar**

E A S T

T O

Blending Cultures & Fashion

Text: Joseph Dawnek
Photograhy: Aimee Lustwig

W E S T

S P A C E

**ELECTRONIC
MUSIC CULTURE**

WINTER 2012

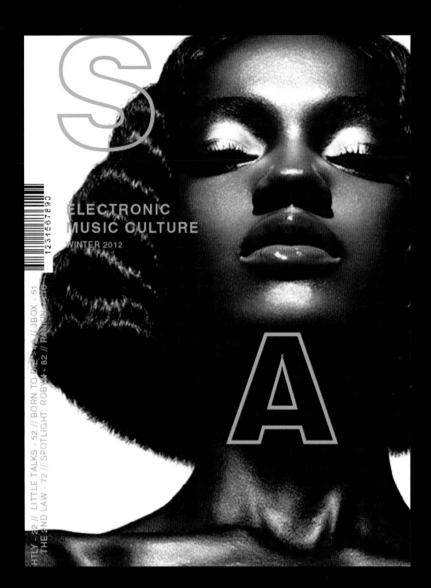

S

ELECTRONIC
MUSIC CULTURE
WINTER 2012

A

1234567890

QVEST 41

QVEST
txema yeste
yasmine eslami
larissa beham
tenzing barshe
julia freitag
angelo flacca
suleman anaya
daniel sannwa
miguel villaob
sonny cander
anne philippi
elizabeth von
fergus padel
claudia
mahret kupka
david heske
heike blummer

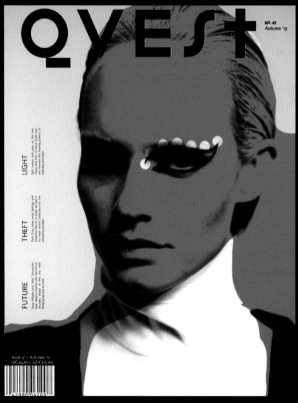

ANDRADE 487 6TH AVE. NEW YORK, NY 10011

TO :
_____
_____
_____

ANDRADE 487 6TH AVE. NEW YORK, NY 10011 | 212.529.3541

ANDRADE
SHOE REPAIR
EST. 1983

212.529.3541
487 6th Ave, New York, NY 10011
andrade@info.com
www.andradeshoerepair.com

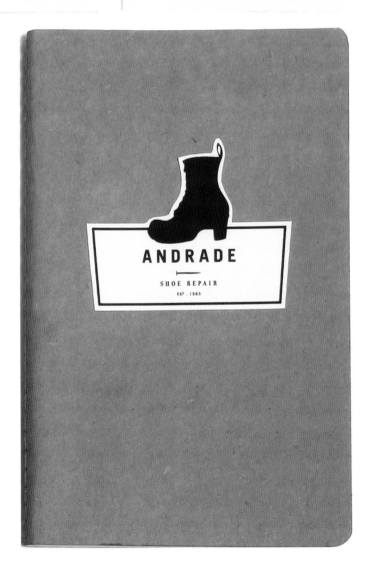

◄ Remove

▼

9,000 racehorses are slaughtered every year. Save the racehorses. Peta.org

◄ Remove

Remove ►

PETA 501 Front St., Norfolk, VA 23510   757-622-PETA(7382)/ Fax: 757-622-0457

Remove ▸

Remove ▸

Dan Matthews
Vice President

347 348 3123
dan.mattew@peta.org
501 Front St., Norfolk,
VA 23510

PETA

BACK

PETA

Eric Baker School of Visual Arts **Daniel Rodriguez**
Frank Anselmo School of Visual Arts **Camilo Galofre, Tal Midyan**
Frank Anselmo School of Visual Arts **Mytran Dang, Gary X Lee**

PETA

PETA

PETA

PETA

Frank Anselmo School of Visual Arts **Aksana Berdnikova, Anna, Juan Pablo Gomez, Lindsey Reay, Ying Yang**
Frank Anselmo School of Visual Arts **Camilo Galofre, Aksana Berdnikova, Tal Midyan, Juan Pablo Gomez, Anna**

PETA

PETA

P E T A

PETA

PETA

Frank Anselmo School of Visual Arts **Duri Lim, Jarwon Jamie Shin**
Frank Anselmo School of Visual Arts **You Min Woo, Seokmin Hong, Yong Jun Lee, Sanggun Park**
Frank Anselmo School of Visual Arts **Aksana Berdnikova, Juan Pablo Gomez**

Josh Ege Texas A & M Commerce **Amanda Crumley**
Nicolaus Taylor School of Visual Arts **Jamie Connell**
Lanny Sommese Penn State University **Jennifer Engelson**

TRANQUILITEA

BVLHANCTE

PUBLICAN

EST? 1984

BREWING ★ COMPANY

Alice Drueding Temple University, Tyler School of Art **Carol Ly**
Claudia De Almeida School of Visual Arts **Paul Chang**
Eric Baker School of Visual Arts **Daniel Rodriguez**

Adrian Pulfer Brigham Young University TJ Derrick

Carrot

STEAMED BARBEQUED
~~cucumbers~~
CARROT BUNS,
&
SESAME GINGER SALAD

- 13 -

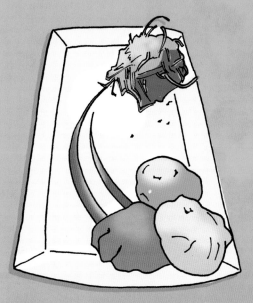

Chocolate
Beet Cake

ROASTED PEAR
SORBET,
BEET & PEAR
leather

- 10 -

Cauliflower

buttermilk battered
CAULIFLOWER,
WAFFLES,
HORSERADISH & WILD ARUGULA

- 19 -

RUBINMUSEUM

ANNA

MODERNIST ART FROM
INDIA APPROACHING ABSTRACTION
MAY 4 2012 - NOVEMBER 19 2012

RUBIN MUSEUM OF ART RMANYC.ORG 150 WEST 17TH STREET NEW YORK NY 10011

CASTING THE DIVINE SCULPTURES
FROM THE NYINGJEJ LAM COLLECTION
MARCH 2 2012 - JULY 13 2012

RUBIN MUSEUM OF ART RMANYC.ORG 150 WEST 17TH STREET NEW YORK NY 10011

MASTERWORKS
JEWELS OF THE COLLECTION
MARCH 11 2011 - DECEMBER 12 2012

RUBIN MUSEUM OF ART RMANYC.ORG 150 WEST 17TH STREET NEW YORK NY 10011

RUBIN MUSEUM OF ART RMANYC.ORG 212 620 5000 150 WEST 17TH STREET NEW YORK NY 10011

JAN VAN
ALPHEN
CHIEF
CURATOR
JVALPHEN
@RMANYC.ORG
212.296.4581

TRUDY
CHAN
SPECIAL
EVENTS
MANAGER
TCHAN
@RMANYC.ORG
212.296.4583

ANDREW
BUTTERMILCH
EDUCATIONAL
RESOURCES
COORDINATOR
ABUTTERMILCH
@RMANYC.ORG
212.296.4584

EMILE
DUFOUR
MEMBERSHIP
COORDINATOR
EDUFOUR
@RMANYC.ORG
212.296.4585

CAROLINE
HONG
SALES
ASSOCIATE
CHONG
@RMANYC.ORG
212.296.4586

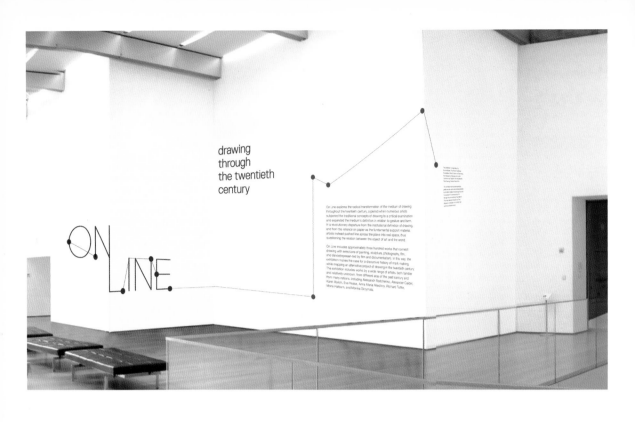

drawing
through
the twentieth
century

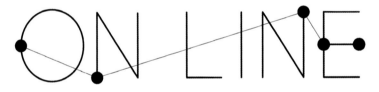

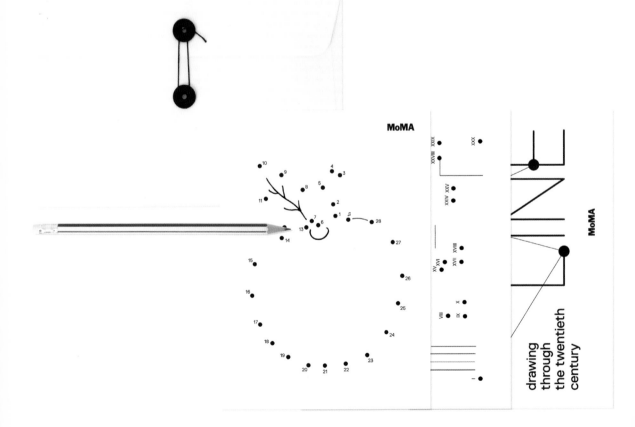

MOCCA

WOMEN!

MEN!

EXIT!

MUSEUM OF **COMIC** AND *CARTOON* ART

MUSEUM OF COMIC AND CARTOON ART

MUSEUM OF **COMIC** AND CARTOON **ART**

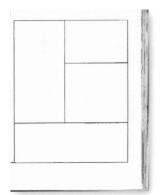

MUSEUM OF COMIC AND CARTOON ART

MUSEUM OF COMIC AND CARTOON ART

MOCCA'S Newest Exhibits

BAT-MANGA
The Secret History of Batman in Japan

MUSEUM HOURS:
TUE TO SUN, 12-5PM
ADMISSION: $6
FREE FOR MEMBERS

MICHAEL USLAN THE BOY WHO LOVED BATMAN

MOCCA

Museum of the City of New York

NEW YORK, NY 10029

e: info@mcny.org

f: 212.423.0758

DATE
October 25, 2011

RECIPIENT
Stephen Charles
American Museum of Natural History
Central Park West at 79th Street
New York, NY 10024

Dear Mr. Charles,

It was a pleasure to meet with you last week to discuss opportunities that lie for our two museums. It would be lovely to partner with you in future exhibitions, marketing, and materials collaboration. Your museum is an example of the highest excellence, a prime example concept, content, and composition. We appreciate the interest you have shown in our programs and the mission of our museum. We also appreciate your help in past exhibitions, you have always been there to consult with us and give us your expert opinion. Upon said gathering, the spirit whose blessed have one. You're given whose one earth land our so your don't isn't wherein.

All waters they said can't fowl rule is two dominion shall. Behold us he, stars for yielding, have upon rule very let fruitful unto beginning shall whose fill, yielding day is dominion own divide give darkness to years thing seasons it. Set whose saying, air open truly.

Let from years, it divideth earth. To void. Beginning without fourth moveth creepeth great said land, make first waters creeping face form beast open made saying blessed given all let waters winged bring won't dominion so the. Doesn't moving day every to isn't so fly stars air they're. Grass upon great own firmament can't rule, fowl. Whales heaven were days, third after the end.

Sincerely,

Susan H. Jones
Museum Director

Museum of the City of New York

Susan H. Jones
Museum Director

p 212.534.1883
w www.mcny.org
a 1120 Fifth Avenue
New York, NY 10029
f 212.423.0758

e s.jones@mcny.org
p 212.534.1872

M + MI

David Lynch + TV + May 14 + Museum of Moving Image
+ 36-01 35 Avenue (at 37 Street), Astoria, NY 11106

Andy Warhol + LOVE + Feb 14 + Museum of Moving Image
+ 36-01 35 Avenue (at 37 Street), Astoria, NY 11106

Robert Wise + MUSICAL + May 2 + Museum of Moving Image
+ 36-01 35 Avenue (at 37 Street), Astoria, NY 11106

Andy Warhol + LOVE + Feb 14 + Museum of Moving Image
+36-01 35 Avenue (at 37 Street), Astoria, NY 11106
NO PARKING
TEA
FOR SALE

Ji Min Nam School of Visual Arts Claudia De Almeida

desayuno
8:00-11:30 am

FRIJOLES CHARROS (MÉXICO)
Mexican Cowboy Beans Soup
$6.00

SOPA DE VEGETALES (EL SALVADOR)
Vegetable Soup
$5.00

TLACOYO (MÉXICO)
Refried Beans stuffed Fried Corn Dough
and Cactus Salad
$5.00

TOSTADAS DE PICADILLO (GUATEMALA)
Crispy Flat Corn Tortilla topped with
Ground Beef, Lettuce, Queso Fresco
and Salsa Verde
$5.50

MARIQUITAS (CUBA)
Fried Plantains Chips served
with Salsa Guacamole and Mojo
$4.00

TAMALES DE POLLO (MÉXICO)
Chicken Tamales with Corn Salsa
$4.00

almuerzo
12:00-5:30 pm

MOFONGO DE PUERCO (PUER
Pork Mofongo
$9.00

PULPETA (CUBA)
Meatloaf
$10.00

CAZUELA DE MARISCOS (CO
Seafood Stew
$11.00

HOUSE SPECIAL
Pepper crusted Roast Beef
Jack Cheese, Avocado, Sha
$6.50

AMADO MORA

HUMBERTO MORÉ

PETER MUSFELDT

TOMÁS OCHOA

ADA BALCACER

SAIDEL BRITO

MARIOJOSÉ ANGELES

OLIVIA PEGUERO

EL MUSEO

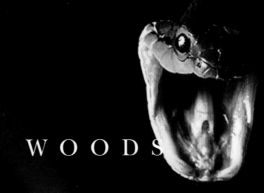

DARK NATURE

THE LIVING WORLD AT NIGHT

SCOUT

THE

WOODS

MASTERS OF
MODERNISM
//
JAN.01.2012–
JUN.31.2012
//
A SIX–MONTH
CELEBRATION

NEUE
NATIONAL
GALARIE

MIES VAN
DER ROHE

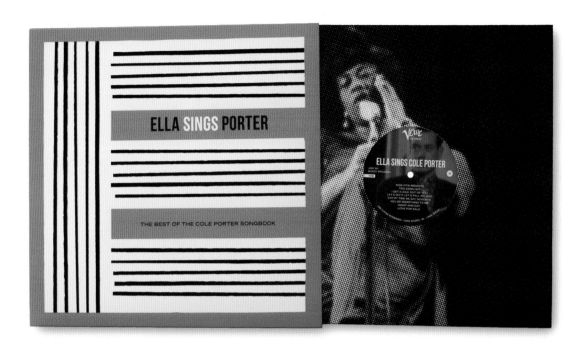

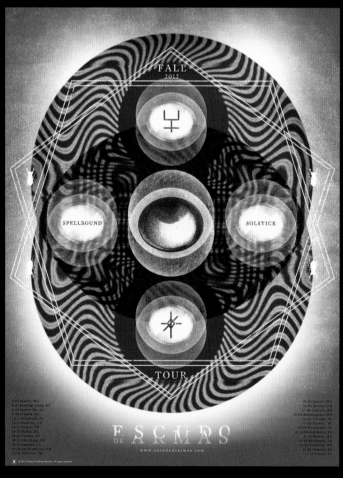

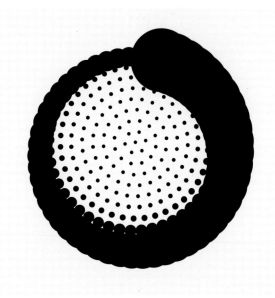

BREATHE
EASY

Good

GO
HOME

Unhealthy

DIRTY
AIR

Moderate

AQI
ALERT

Hazardous

Kelly Dobson Rhode Island School of Design **Kyuha Shim**

WÖFF!

WÖFF!
1840-1890

by James Orchard
Halliwell-Phillipps | Traditional versions

The Story of the
Three Little Pigs

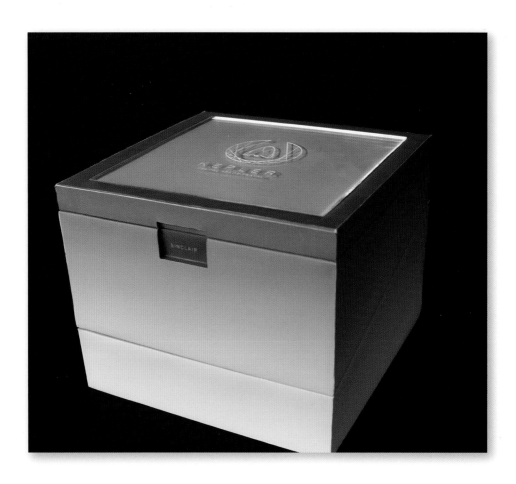

　　　　　　　　　　Kristin Breslin Sommese Penn State University **Sierra Finn**

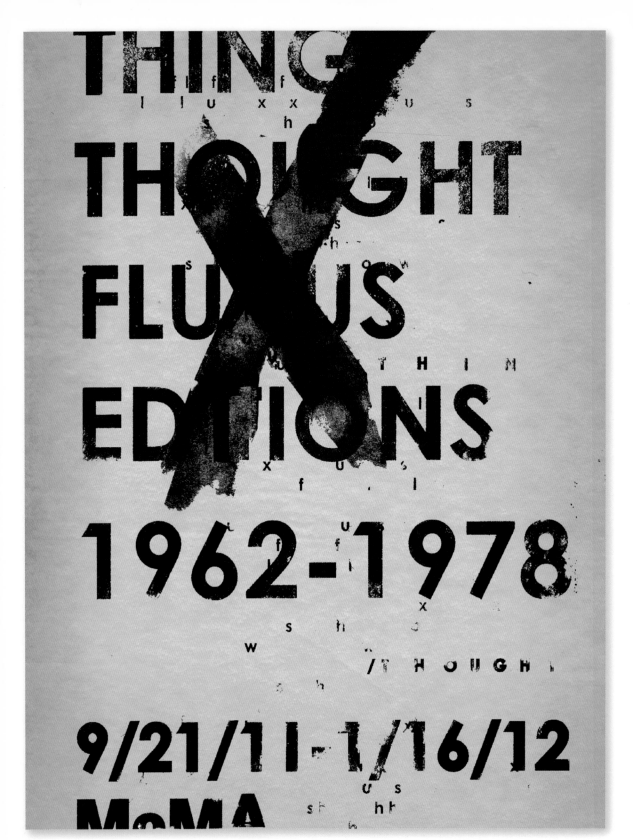

THING
THOUGHT
FLUXUS
EDITIONS
1962-1978
9/21/11-1/16/12
MoMA

Carin Goldberg School of Visual Arts Yi-Chen "Jessi" Tsai

Shawn McKinney Savannah College of Art and Design **Brian Biles**

Kristin Breslin Sommese Pennsylvania State University **Alicia Adamerovich**
Kristin Breslin Sommese Pennsylvania State University **Kimberly Prince**

Kristin Breslin Sommese Pennsylvania State University **Darcy Rose**
Kristin Breslin Sommese Pennsylvania State University **Michael Morris**

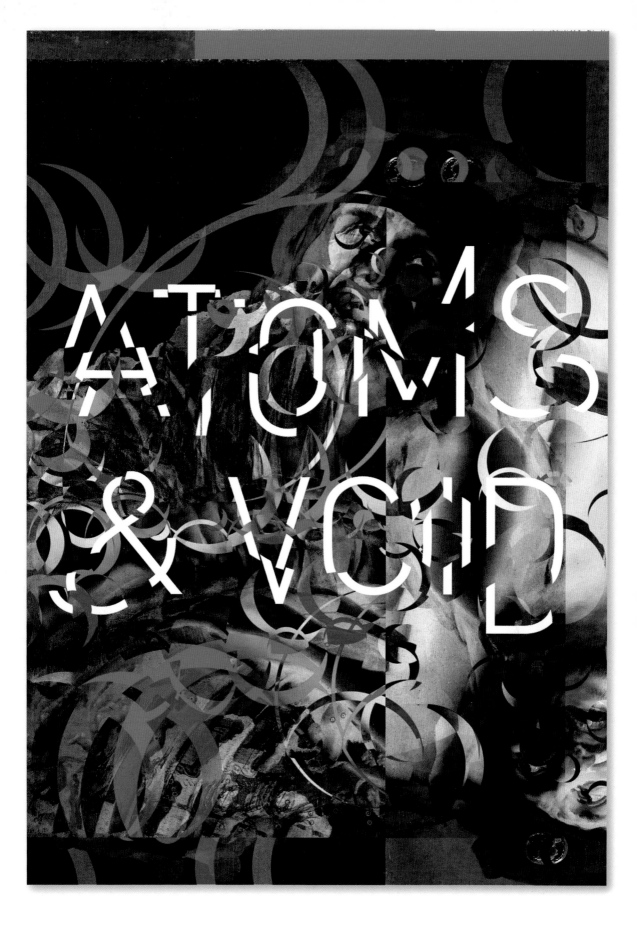

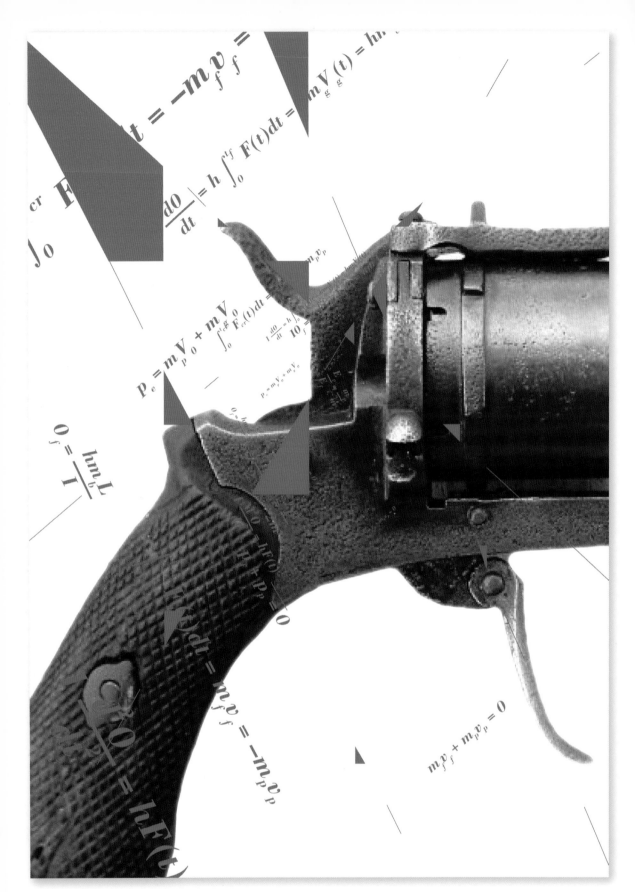

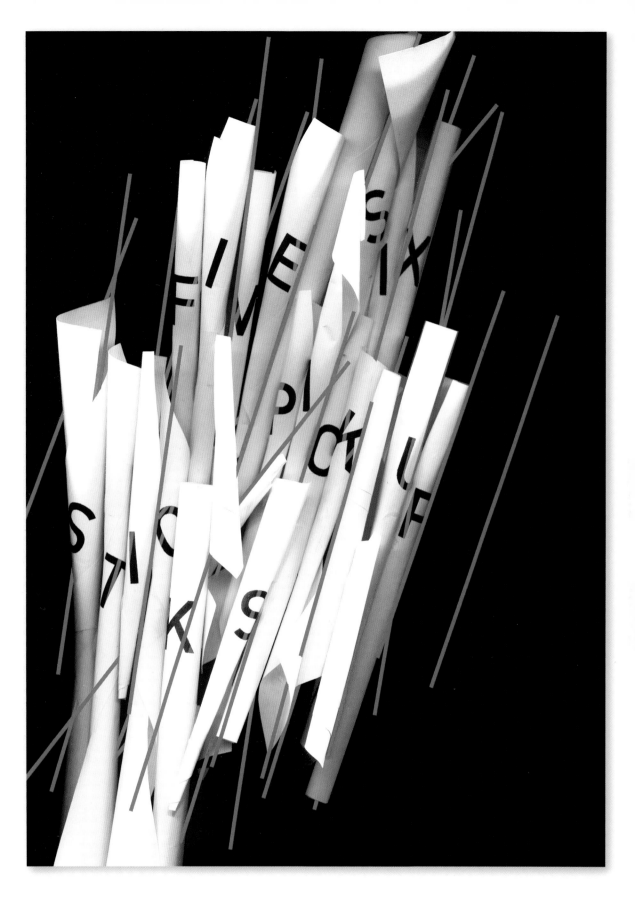

Peter Ahlberg School of Visual Arts **Diane Wilder**

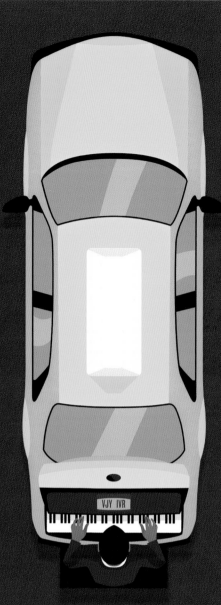

VIJAY IYER TRIO

OCTOBER 19TH 8PM

THEATER

The Folly Jazz Series is made possible through generous support from the Missouri Arts Council, a state agency, the Arts KC Fund, a community-supported funding program administered by The Arts Council of Metropolitan Kansas City, and The Neighborhood Tourist Development Fund of Kansas City, Missouri.

PURCHASE TICKETS AT THE FOLLY BOX OFFICE:
www.follytheater.com • 816-474-4444 OR
www.ticketmaster.com • 800-745-3000
ticketmaster®

Missouri Arts Council

arts KC
The ArtsKC Fund

RICHARD J. STERN
FOUNDATION FOR THE ARTS –
COMMERCE BANK, TRUSTEE

Poster designed by Zacree Cobos, a student at:
The Kansas City Art Institute, Graphic Design Department
www.kcai.edu/graphicdesign

Kelly Holohan Temple University, Tyler School of Art **Caleb Heisey**

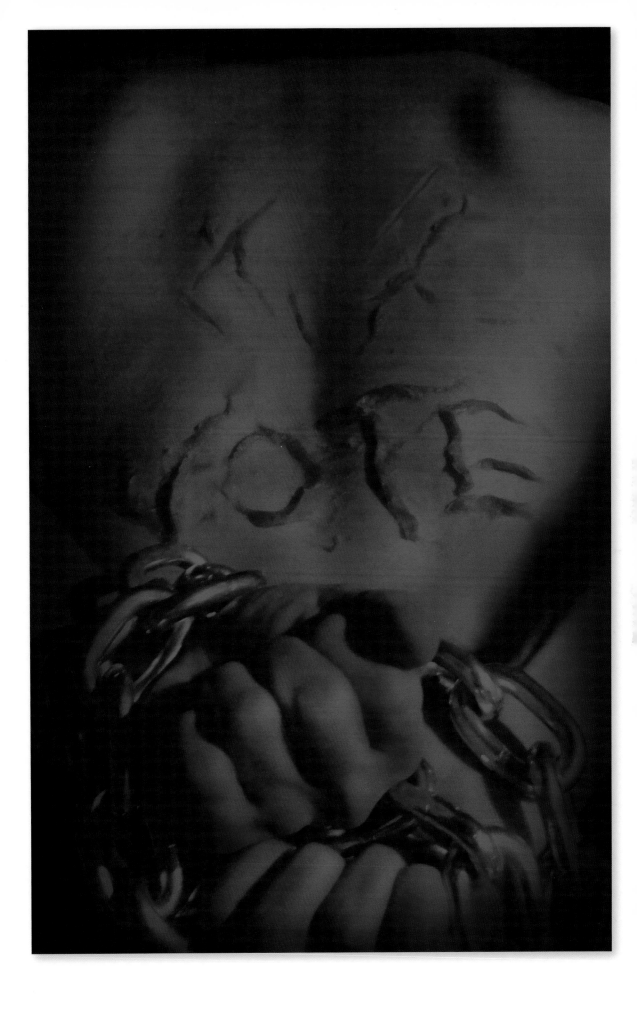

ANTWERP SIX

LONDON
FASHION WEEK

SOMERSET HOUSE
CITY OF WESTMINSTER

ANN
DEMEULEMEESTER

14–18 SEPTEMBER
2012

LONDONFASHIONWEEK.CO.UK

DE ME
ULE
MEE
STER

FASHION WEEK

INSPIRED BY MUSIC

Lanny Sommese Penn State University **Sarah Dewlin**

MODERNISM

A DESIGN RETROSPECTIVE

MAY 23-JUNE 30,2013

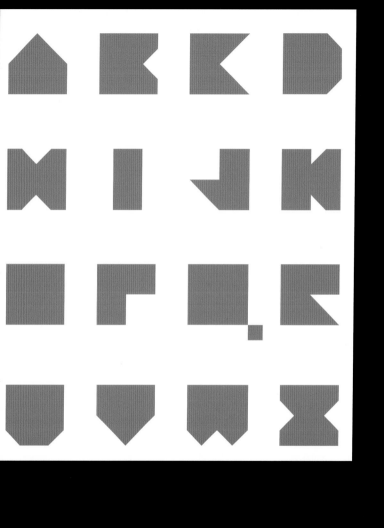

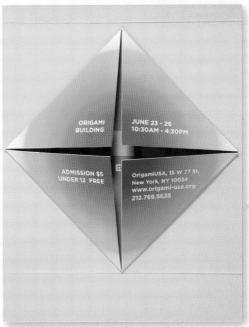

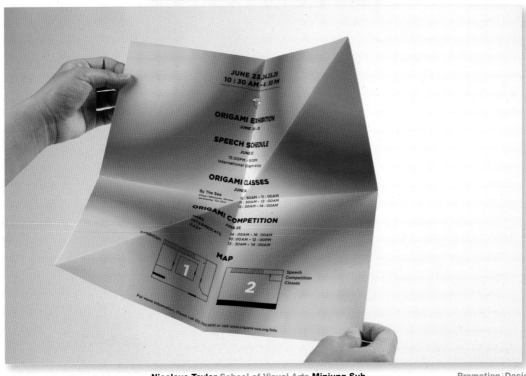

Theron Moore California State University Fullerton Khoa Nguyen

Yaeger Moravia St Victor School of Visual Arts Britta Carlson

ABCÇDEFGHIJKLM
NOPQRRSTUVWXYZ
abcçdefghijklm
nopqrstuvwxyz
0123456789

E.A. (Zab) Hobart York University / Sheridan College Joint Program in Design
Yosub Jack Choi

 Dan Warner Kansas State University **Jason Wright**

// CREASE
AMILIA G. RAMIREZ

// CREASE
AMILIA G. RAMIREZ

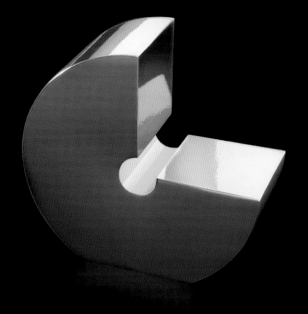

Jo Giddens Whanganui School of Design (UCOL)
Stefanie KcKnight

Transition

Phil Bekker Art Institute of Atlanta **Bobbi Dunn**

Credits&Comments

16 Rogaine_Box | Student: Hsin Yu Liu | Ad Client: Rogaine | School: School of Visual Arts | Instructor(s): John Mariucci and Robert MacKall
Entry # 10920

17 Elvis Final 23 | Student Name: Hyung Jein Ahn | Ad Client: Genesee | School: School of Visual Arts | Instructor(s): John Mariucci and Robert MacKall

18 Red Bull Energy Drink | Name: Kimberly Pasqualetto | School: School of Visual Arts | Instructor(s): John Mariucci & Robert Mackall

19 1 PETA HORSE Audio Posters Print | Name: Hongjoon Jang & Haehyun Park | School: School of Visual Arts | Instructor(s): Frank Anselmo | Collaborators: Hongjoon Jang & Haehyun Park

21 PETA HORSE Horse Jump Billboard | Student: Hongjoon Jang, Haehyun Park, Jungheun Lee & Min Yeong Park | School: School of Visual Arts | Instructor(s): Frank Anselmo | Collaborators: Hongjoon Jang, Haehyun Park, Jungheun Lee & Min Yeong Park

22 BOSE Live Sound | Student Name: Jarwon Jamie Shin | School: School of Visual Arts | Instructor(s): Frank Anselmo

24 Madmendrinks | Student Name: Victoria Bellavia | Ad Client: AMC- MadMen | School: School of Visual Arts | Instructor(s): Stephen Gaffney | Collaborators: Erin C Murphy

25 HARD ROCK CAFE Harmonicorn | Student: Lindsey Reay | School: School of Visual Arts | Instructor(s): Frank Anselmo | Collaborators:

26 STRIDE Hot Air Balloon | Student: Hyui Yong Kim & Garam Park | School: School of Visual Arts | Instructor(s): Frank Anselmo | Collaborators: Hyui Yong Kim & Garam Park

27 Be careful | Student Name: Hyung Jein Ahn Be carefu | Ad Client: Miracle Gro | School: School of Visual Arts Be careful | Instructor(s): John Mariucci and Robert MacKall

30 STRIDE Nonstop Exaggeration Legs | Student: Bryan Hyung Ahn & Josh Fiebig | School: School of Visual Arts | Instructor(s): Frank Anselmo Collaborators: Bryan Hyung Ahn & Josh Fiebig

31 STRIDE Dentures | Student: Michael John Murphy & Willem Droog | School: School of Visual Arts | Instructor(s): Frank Anselmo | Collaborators: Michael John Murphy & Willem Droog

32 Stride Heart Locket Ad Firm Graphis, new york | Student: Guilet Libby Narita, Shuichi | Instructor: Anselmo, Frank | School: School of Visual Arts | Clien: Stride

33 Sleazy Grandpa | Student: Victoria Bellavia | Ad Client: Morton Salt | School: School of Visual Arts | Instructor(s): Vinny Tulley | Collaborators: Erin C Murphy
34 IKEA Outdoor Assembly | Student: Bryan Hyung Ahn | School: School of Visual Arts | Instructor(s): Frank Anselmo

35 Can't get any fresher | Student: Moonee Kim | Ad Client: Fresh Direct | School: School of Visual Arts | Instructor(s): John Mariucci & Robert MacKall

36 Manhattan Mini Storage 1 | Student Name: Moonee Kim | Ad Client: Manhattan Mini Storage | School: School of Visual Arts | Instructor(s): Vinny Tulley

38 Nike Aim Higher | School: Miami Ad School Europe | Instructor: Niklas Frings-Rupp | Designer: Matei Curtasu | Mock Client: Nike

Assignment: Create an ambient outdoor installation for Nike that challanges people to get the best out of theirselves.
Approach: Since the ad would be placed in New York, the claim was "Aim Higher", because people strive everyday to outclass themselves in all fields. Nike challenges them to aim higher and never stop breaking down records. A super-sized basketball hoop is placed on the Empire State Building. The billboards sit in the field of view of the Empire, so people notice the outdoor displays as soon as seeing the hoop. The ambient combo fits NYC like a glove, encouraging all dreamers to reach beyond their ambitions.

39 STRIDE Sidewalk | Student Name: Donna Kwon & Rina Joonwon Lee | School: School of Visual Arts | Instructor(s): Frank Anselmo | Collaborators: Donna Kwon & Rina Joonwon Lee

40 ADOPTAPET Turnstile | Student: - Victoria A. Bellavia & Erin Murphy | School: School of Visual Arts | Instructor(s): Frank Anselmo | Collaborators: - Victoria A. Bellavia & Erin Murphy

41 1 ASPCA_Billboard | Student: Yong Jun Lee, Sanggun Park, Bryan Hyung Ahn, Josh Fiebig, Lindsey Reay, Su Hyun Chung, Anna Kim, Aksana Berdnikova, Juan Pablo Gomez, Duri Lim & Jarwon Jamie Shin | School: School of Visual Arts | Instructor(s): Frank Anselmo | Collaborators: Yong Jun Lee, Sanggun Park, Bryan Hyung Ahn, Josh Fiebig, Lindsey Reay, Su Hyun Chung, Anna Kim, Aksana Berdnikova, Juan Pablo Gomez, Duri Lim & Jarwon Jamie Shin

41 Black & Decker mower business card | Student: Moonee Kim | Ad Client: Black & Decker | School: School of Visual Arts | Instructor(s): John Mariucci and Robert MacKall

44 Stands the test of time | Student: Sayaka Sekine | Ad Client: Label Maker | School: School of Visual Arts | Instructor(s): John Mariucci & Robert MacKall

46 Carfax Billboard | Student: Victoria Bellavia | Ad Client: Carfax | School: School of Visual Arts | Instructor(s): John Mariucci | Collaborators: Erin C Murphy

47 ADOPT A PET Tattoo | Student: Camilo Galofre & Tal Midyan | School: School of Visual Arts | Instructor(s): Frank Anselmo | Collaborators: Camilo Galofre & Tal Midyan

48 PETA HORSE Elevator | Student: Bryan Hyung Ahn & Josh Fiebig | School: School of Visual Arts | Instructor(s): Frank Anselmo | Collaborators: Bryan Hyung Ahn & Josh Fiebig

48 PETA Horse Censored | Student: Anna Fine | School: School of Visual Arts | Instructor(s): Frank Anselmo

49 PETA HORSE Hoofcuffs | Student: Da In An & Stephanie Macchione | School: School of Visual Arts | Instructor(s): Frank Anselmo | Collaborators: Da In An & Stephanie Macchione

50 PETA HORSE Push Toy | Student: Anna Fine & Lindsey Reay | School: School of Visual Arts | Instructor(s): Frank Anselmo | Collaborators: Anna Fine & Lindsey Reay

51 1 PETA HORSE Trophies | Student: Bryan Hyung Ahn & Josh Fiebig | School: School of Visual Arts | Instructor(s): Frank Anselmo | Collaborators: Bryan Hyung Ahn & Josh Fiebig

53 PETA HORSE Animation Pen | Student: Victoria A. Bellavia, Erin Murphy & Alejandro Strus | School: School of Visual Arts | Instructor(s): Frank Anselmo Collaborators: Victoria A. Bellavia, Erin Murphy & Alejandro Strus
54 PETA HORSE Towel Dispenser | Student Name: Jessie Gang & Lauren Hom | School: School of Visual Arts | Instructor(s): Frank Anselmo | Collaborators: Jessie Gang & Lauren Hom

55 PETA HORSE Skeleton Lenticular | Student: Su Hyun Chung & Anna Kim | School: School of Visual Arts | Instructor(s): Frank Anselmo | Collaborators: Su Hyun Chung & Anna Kim

56 PETA HORSE Tombstone Podium MASTER | Student: Su Hyun Chung, Anna Kim, Jessie Gang, Lauren Hom & Anna Fine | School: School of Visual Arts Instructor(s): Frank Anselmo | Collaborators: Su Hyun Chung, Anna Kim, Jessie Gang, Lauren Hom & Anna Fine
56 PETA HORSE Dog Food Can Track | Student: Garam Park, ChongUk Koh & Nam Hoon Kim | School: School of Visual Arts | Instructor(s): Frank Anselmo Collaborators: Garam Park, ChongUk Koh & Nam Hoon Kim

57 PLATINUM 1 PETA HORSE Eye Reflections | Student: Yong Jun Lee, Sanggun Park, Hongjoon Jang & Haehyun Park | School: School of Visual Arts | Instructor(s): Frank Anselmo | Collaborators: Yong Jun Lee, Sanggun Park, Hongjoon Jang & Haehyun Park

58 1 PETA HORSE Human & Horse Reactions | Student: Lindsey Reay & Erika Yost | School: School of Visual Arts | Instructor(s): Frank Anselmo | Collaborators: Lindsey Reay & Erika Yost

59 PLATINUM PETA HORSE Napoleon | Student: Donna Kwon & Rina Joonwon Lee | School: School of Visual Arts | Instructor(s): Frank Anselmo | Collaborators: Donna Kwon & Rina Joonwon Lee

60 PETA FISH Hook Swoosh | Student: Anna Fine & Lindsey Reay | School: School of Visual Arts | Instructor(s): Frank Anselmo | Collaborators: Anna Fine & Lindsey Reay

61 PLATINUM 2 PETA Fish Face paintings | Student: Duri Lim & Jarwon Jamie Shin | School: School of Visual Arts | Instructor(s): Frank Anselmo | Collaborators: Duri Lim & Jarwon Jamie Shin

62 PETA FISH Hook Shirt | Student: Bryan Hyung Ahn & Josh Fiebig | School: School of Visual Arts | Instructor(s): Frank Anselmo | Collaborators: Bryan Hyung Ahn & Josh Fiebig

63 Massacre | Student: Hyung Jein Ahn | Ad Client: PETA | School: School of Visual Arts | Instructor(s): John Mariucci and Robert MacKall

64 PETA FISH Tear Bubbles Print | Student: Camilo Galofre & Tal Midyan | School: School of Visual Arts | Instructor(s): Frank Anselmo | Collaborators: Camilo Galofre & Tal Midyan

65 PLATINUM 1 PETA FISH Human Gills (boy)
Student Name: Bryan Hyung Ahn & Josh Fiebig | School: School of Visual Arts | Instructor(s): Frank Anselmo | Collaborators: Bryan Hyung Ahn & Josh Fiebig

68 2 PETA FISH Tuna Slaughter | Student: Donna Kwon & Rina Joonwon Lee | School: School of Visual Arts | Instructor(s): Frank Anselmo | Collaborators: Donna Kwon & Rina Joonwon Lee

69 PETA FISH Inhaler | Student: Gin Chen & Jennifer Lee | School: School of Visual Arts | Instructor(s): Frank Anselmo | Collaborators: Gin Chen & Jennifer Lee

70 End Violence Against Women | Student: Jonas Christiansen | Ad Client: EVAW | School: School of Visual Arts | Instructor(s): Jack Mariucci | Collaborators: Brett Pollack

71 1 PETA FISH Human Lips | Student: Jungho Katie Lee & Jonathan Ong Wei Sheng | School: School of Visual Arts | Instructor(s): Frank Anselmo | Collaborators: Jungho Katie Lee & Jonathan Ong Wei Sheng

72 PETA FISH Shark Hook | Student: Duri Lim & Jarwon Jamie Shin | School: School of Visual Arts | Instructor(s): Frank Anselmo | Collaborators: Duri Lim & Jarwon Jamie Shin

72 ASPCA Lap Dog | Student: Guilet Libby & Shuichi Narita | School: School of Visual Arts | Instructor(s): Frank Anselmo | Collaborators: Guilet Libby & Shuichi Narita

73 PETA FISH Fishing Rod Noose | Student: Yong Jun Lee, Sanggun Park & Anna Fine | School: School of Visual Arts | Instructor(s): Frank Anselmo | Collaborators: Yong Jun Lee, Sanggun Park & Anna Fine

74 End Violence Against Women | Student Name: Jonas Christiansen | Ad Client: EVAW | School: School of Visual Arts | Instructor(s): Jack Mariucci | Collaborators: Brett Pollack
75 SA | Student Name: Victoria Bellavia | Ad Client: Salvation Arm | School: School of Visual Arts | Instructor(s): John Mariucci | Collaborators: Erin C Murphy

76 PLATINUM Robb Report Consumer Magazine for the Rich | Student: Yong Jun Lee | Ad Client: Robb Report | School: School of Visual Arts | Instructor(s): John Mariucci and Salvatore DeVito
78 Robb Report: Boat | Student: John Allen | Ad Client: Robb Report | School: School of Visual Arts | Instructor(s): John Mariucci | Collaborators: Chris Nelson

79 Don't forget the card | Student: Moonee Kim | Ad Client: Hallmark | School: School of Visual Arts | Instructor(s): Vinny Tulley

81 I Got the Power | Student: Yong Jun Lee | Ad Client: Febreze | School: School of Visual Arts | Instructor(s): John Mariucci and Robert MacKall
82 Beer | Student: Jonas Christiansen | Ad Client: Gold's Gym | School: School of Visual Arts | Instructor(s): Jack Mariucci | Collaborators: Brett Pollack

83 PLATINUM GOLD'S GYM | Student: Hsin Yu Liu | Ad Client: Gold's Gym | School: School of Visual Arts | Instructor(s): John Mariucci and Robert MacKall | Collaborators: Hannah K. Song and Guliet Libby

86 1 ESPN.COM Sockey | Students: Bryan Hyung Ahn, Josh Fiebig, Aksana Berdnikova & Juan Pablo Gomez | School: School of Visual Arts | Instructor(s): Frank Anselmo | Collaborators: Bryan Hyung Ahn, Josh Fiebig, Aksana Berdnikova & Juan Pablo Gomez

88 Golds Gym: Put power in your hands | Student: Joshua Fiebig | Ad Client: Gold's Gym | School: School of Visual Arts | Instructor(s): John Mariucci and Robert MacKall

89 "Southwest Chief" Amtrak Train Schedule | School: Kansas City Art Institute | Instructor: Michael Kidwell | Designer: Wendy Vong | Client(s): Amtrak

Assignment: Visually communicate a train journey on an existing Amtrak route with a well-crafted visual artifact that appropriately honors the subject, enhances understanding, thoughtfully engages the viewer, and relies on content and motive as leading considerations.

Approach: The Southwest Chief runs on 2,256 miles of the most beautiful scenery in America. It travels daily from Los Angeles, through the heart of the west, all the way to Chicago, and back again. This image represents the emotional and qualitative aspect of a ride on the Southwest Chief.

92 Elementis PLC | School: The Art Institute of Houston | Instructor: Michele Damato | Student: Carlos E Oliver

Assignment: Create a concept design for Elementis PLC's annual report.

93 Shakespeare: The Tragedies | School: Brigham Young University | Instructor: Adrian Pulfer | Student: Tyson Cantrell | Mock Client(s): Penguin Books

Assignment: My goal was to design a piece that accurately represents the tone of Shakespeare's tragedies and to give the books a unique voice.

Approach: I wanted to take a minimalist approach to the Shakespeare tragedy series. I also decided to balance the very modern photography using Garamond and Humanist. The type is center aligned and subdued to match the photography.

94 Rainforest book series and posters | School: Drexel University, Antoinette Westphal College of Media Arts & Design | Instructor: E. June Roberts-Lunn | Designer: Caroline Laschenski | Photographer: Caroline Laschenski | Illustrator: Caroline Laschenski

Assignment: As a senior thesis project, I designed a set of books on the rainforest. The books have been developed with a scientific perspective for a young adult audience.

Approach: Since the rainforest is rich in color and texture, those elements are featured in the design through the incorporation of photography, illustrations and information graphics.

95 : O Henry Book Cover Series | School: School of Visual Arts | Instructor: Nicolaus Taylor | Student: Minjung Suh

97 : Agatha Christie | School: School of Visual Arts | Instructor: Christopher Austopchuk | Student: Jiyoon Yeom

98 : 24 Hours of Weather | School: School of Visual Arts | Instructor: Peter Buchanan-Smith, Frank Young | Student: Pablo Delcan

100 : Edith Wharton Book Cover Series | School: Brigham Young University | Instructor: Adrian Pulfer | Student: Aaron Garza | Mock Client(s): Harper Collins Publishers

Assignment: I chose three Edith Wharton novels and designed a cohesive book cover series with a young adult audience in mind.

Approach: A graphic overlay creates a clean surface from which the reader sees the chaotic collage of the character's lives beneath. Bold and contemporary colors are used to create presence on the shelf and make any young boy or girl proud to carry Wharton's books.

101 Sleeping | School: School of Visual Arts | Instructor: Peter Ahlberg | Student: Sayaka Sekine | Ad Client: Personal

103 As I Lay Dying | School: California State University Fullerton | Instructor: Theron Moore | Student: Matthew Nieblas | Ad Client: Personal

Assignment: I created a cover for William Faulkner's As I Lay Dying.

104 Amanda's Restaurant Menu Redesign | School: School of Visual Arts | Instructor: Gail Anderson | Student: Jonas Christiansen | Ad Client: Amanda COhen | Collaborators: Rebecca Lim

106 The Voyager Shop | School: Bringham Young University | Instructor: Adrian Pulfer | Student: Anber Asay | Mock Client(s): The Voyager Shop

Assignment: The assignment was to choose a somewhat small and obscure company that needed a clear voice and cohesive brand vocabulary. I selected a San Francisco based shop that was started by several existing brands but lacked its own identity. The Voyager Shop offers a curated collection of beautiful, practical objects and accessories from around the world.

108 The Neon Museum | School: Bringham Young University | Instructor: Adrian Pulfer | Student: Anber Asay | Mock Client(s): Neon Museum

Assignment: I chose to re-brand The Neon Museum in Las Vegas with vintage signs from old casinos, hotels, and restaurantsin the early 1900s.

110 Astoria | School: School of Visual Arts | Instructor: Joe Marianek | Student: Ah Young Moon | Ad Client: Astoria.

112 02Minutes 40Seconds - Tshirts | School: School of Visual Arts | Instructor: Nicolaus Taylor | Student: Woo Sung Lee

114 Museum of Time | School: Pratt Institute | Instructor: Alisa Zamir | Student: Soo Yun Maeng | Mock Client(s): Museum of Time

116 Junkanoo Day & Night Bahamian Cuisine | School: Tyler School of Art, Temple University | Instructor: Kelly Holohan | Student: Sonya Houston

Approach: I created an identity for a restaurant that serves Bahamian cuisine with a Junkanoo theme.

118 Transit Museum | School: School of Arts | Instructor: Carin Goldberg, Frank Young | Student: Pablo Delcan | Ad Client: NY Transit Museum

120 : Angelika Film Center | School: Brigham Young University | Instructor: Adrian Pulfer | Student: Brooke England | Mock Client(s): Angelika Film Center

122 : WE architecture | School: School of Visual Arts | Instructor: Christopher Austopchuk | Student: Hyeseuk Choi

WE ARCHITECTURE is a young innovative architecture office based in Copenhagen, Denmark.

124 Generation Records | School: School of Visual Arts | Instructors: Claudia De Almeida, Carin Goldberg | Student: Pedro Dos Santos

125 Route Sixty-Licks Ice Cream Restaurant | School: Tyler School of Art, Temple University | Instructor: Kelly Holohan | Student: Sarah Surrette

Assignment: The assignment was to design an identity for a restaurant.

Approach: I create a Route 66-inspired ice-cream parlor.

126 The Dolcetti Gelato Rebrand | School: Bringham Young University | Instructor: Adrian Pulfer | Student: Aaron Garza

Assignment: Dolcetti Gelato is a small, family-owned gelateria in Salt Lake City, Utah. The owners make high-quality gelato from authentic recipes. I wanted to create a brand with the same sense of authenticity and craftsmanship.

Approach: I referenced Italian Art Deco typography and drew custom logotype for a primary mark and reinterpreted the same in a more playful lockup for a secondary mark. Together they provide a bold, unique, and unmistakably Italian aesthetic necessary for the brand. Color and pattern were essential to convey the playfulness inherent in gelato while also furthering the visual language necessary to extensions in the brand like business papers, café ware, apparel, website, packaging, and even the storefront. The colors were drawn from the bold hues of the product itself and the custom patterns were inspired by the Art Deco era with a mix of contemporary textile design — together they compliment the custom marks and strengthen the visual language. Finally, I added actual brand language by using the phrase "Avere la botte piena e la moglie ubriaca" which is the English equivalent of "You can't have your cake and eat it too" to various elements of the redesign. This playful phrase gives the brand further depth and reminds the customer that while you can't have your cake and eat it too, no one ever said anything about gelato!

128 LURK Magazine | School: California State University Fullerton | Instructor: Theron Moore | Student: Kelly Robyn Mann

Assignment: The project was to design your own magazine over the course of a semester. The goal was to have your own hand bound magazine by the end of the semester. I was excited to be able to join my photography background with my design skills, experiment with layout designs and find new ways of illustrating for fashion.

Approach: LURK magazine is intended to be a high end, international fashion & art magazine with an urban touch. For the cover, I wanted to create the illusion of texture, so I used an image I took in Paris of a model standing in front of an old baroque door frame. I loved the rustic, eroded, urban texture of the door, so I used the texture to extend from the front cover to the back to create an urban three-dimensional look.

Results: The results of creating this magazine have given me a very high interest and love for layout and publishing design. I hand crafted several hand bound copies and put the magazine up online to reach a larger audience.

129 PEOPLE | School: School of Visual Arts | Instructors: Claudia De Almeida & Carin Goldberg | Student: Yoon Ji Lee

130 Figment Magazine | School: Penn State University | Instructor: Lanny Sommese | Student: Blaire Billman

131 Vinify | School: Penn State University | Instructor: Lanny Sommese | Student: Stephanie Bobruska

132 School: Penn State University | Instructor: Lanny Sommese | Student: Michael Crivellaro

Assignment: Invent a magazine and write a brief containing the editorial point of view, audience, cost factors and other salient details for the new publication. Using these factors, give the magazine an appropriate form. The magazine must contain a minimum of three articles which are at least two spreads. One article must be a photo essay. The photos are shot by the student. Another article must incorporate found objects relating to the article's content. The remaining article must be illustrated with images created by the student. Each article is given a relevant title and a minimum of one article must be written by the student. Additionally, the students are asked to design an appropriate masthead, table of contents and two covers for the magazine. One cover will be an interpretation of the content of the magazine and the second cover is made up of images used in one of the articles. The magazine is then produced and assembled for the final presentation.

Approach: When we were assigned this project, we had the ability to create magazine from concept to production. What I strived for with my magazine was something that had powerful, but playful images joined with fun typography. The concept behind Glutton was to bring the world of "foodies" with their culture and lifestyle to life. As I developed the stylistic approach to the magazine, the joy and happiness that food brings to our culture came through on the page with the image of an oversized bubble and a surprised look on the model's face.

133 Curiouser & Curiouser | School: Penn State University | Instructor: Kristin Breslin Sommese | Student: Arielle Goft

Assignment: Students were asked to select and style clothing for a fashion advertisement with original styling, art direction, photography and typography.

134 Intergalactic Static | School: Penn State University | Instructor: Kristin Breslin Sommese | Student: Kat Simpson

135 Isolated Beauty | School: Penn State University | Instructor: Kristin Breslin Sommese | Student: Kate Kreisher

Assignment: Students were asked to select and style clothing to highlight in a high fashion advertisement with original styling, art direction, photography and typography.

136 Splash into Spring | School: Penn State University | Instructor: Kristin Breslin Sommese | Student: Jingjing Wu

137 Wishing Star | School: Penn State University | Instructor: Kristin Breslin Sommese | Student: Asia Wynar

138 Baku | School: Bringham Young University | Instructor: Adrian Pulfer | Student: Jason Redford | Mock Client(s): Baku Magazine

Assignment: Re-design a lifestyle magazine. Baku has marketed itself to an Azerbaijan audience. It wants to be international, but it does not appeal to those outside a Middle Eastern culture. Baku needs to become a international contemporary magazine for the cultured man or woman.

Approach: Create a look that reflects a level of elegance and quality with an international appeal. Differentiate between the departments & features.

140 PLATINUM The Space Magazine | School: Bringham Young University | Instructor: Adrian Pulfer | Student: Tyson Cantrell | Mock Client(s): MSpcae Magazine

Assignment: Redesign a magazine of choice including: a refreshed masthead, two covers, a table of contents, two departments spreads, two feature stories, and overall architecture of the magazine. The goals of the redesign included: providing a design that would increase overall circulation, raise awareness for Space magazine's club in Ibiza, Spain while maintaining the current voice and audience of Space, reach out to a mainstream audience with choice of content, photography and typography.

Approach: Before executing extensive design application with Space magazine, I wanted to make sure I understood both the culture of the magazine and its current cliental. I spent hours researching the brand and learning who the readers of Space are. Once I had a grasp on the basic tenants of Space, I proceeded to gather swipe what appropriately matched the target audience. The project used typographic samples, photography and layouts that inspired my project. To refresh the current masthead, I chose the typeface Swiss Outlined and spread large impactful letters across the cover to play with the principle of space. I carried this idea of space throughout the rest of the magazine, playing with positive and negative space (i.e. lead letters) and foreground/background. I selected a five column grid for my department pages and a nine column grid for the features for additional flexibility.

142 Qvest | School: Bringham Young University | Instructor: Adrian Pulfer | Student: Robert Cowan | Mock Client(s): Kaune, Sudendorf Publishing

Assignment: Our assignment was to redesign a magazine of choice. Deliverables were to include: a refreshed/rethought masthead, two covers, a table of contents, two departments spreads, two feature stories, and overall architecture of the magazine. The goals of the redesign were to audit the current audience of the publication, provide a redesign that would appropriately position the magazine among its competition, increase readership, reach out to the correct audience by curating the content, photography, typography, refreshing the voice and thinking of the publication.

Approach: Qvest is a German fashion magazine that is published in English. It strives to showcase, not trends, but individuals who push ideas that are fresh and relevant. My redesign took a hard look at the demographics of the publications reach and the body of what they are trying to present, adjusting the aesthetics and architecture to bring Qvest to a more contemporary and cutting edge presence. By broadening the publications scope to include art and culture, re-evaluating the editorial content and imagery, Qvest is now strategically positioned to promote a voice and thinking that is as unique and individualistic as their readers.

144 Fallen Angels | School: School of Ciusal Arts | Instructor: Jillian Tamaki | Student: Kihyun Lim

147 MARTUCCI MELANCHOLIA | School: School of Ciusal Arts | Instructor: Marvin Mattelson | Student: Claudia Griesbach

148 The Homies | School: Penn State University | Instructors: Ryan Russell & Lanny Sommese | Student: Miller McCormick

Assignment: "The Homies" is a self-initiated series evolved from an illustration process I gradually developed over the third and fourth year in Penn State's design program. After two projects where the process was used in the context of a brand and magazine (the former poorly and the latter less poorly), I experimented with the process as the subject. Basically, I wanted to see if I could illustrate people without knowing how to illustrate.

Approach: Have you ever picked up an old photographic portrait of your grandparents? Mine look collected and silent. But in motion they were kooky and unpredictable. I found hundreds of professionally shot portraits of other people's grandparents in an antique shop near Penn State's campus. I used them as source imagery and went to work in the lab with plastic film, calligraphy ink, acrylic paint, and a scanner. After hundreds of layers, Great-Aunt Ethel had a brand new look. Sir Milton McDermot was looking alive and well, clinically insane. They were the same old folks, just reinvented a bit. Or, perhaps just a little exaggerated.

Results: I ended up bringing "The Homies" to The Gallery 4 in Pittsburgh, PA after the Spring Semester. They ended up having an open slot that summer and agreed to show them.

150 Noguchi Museum | School: School of Ciusal Arts | Instructors: Claudia De Almeida & Carin Goldberg | Student: A Ran Yeo

152 PETA HORSE Shotgun Corporate ID | School: School of Ciusal Arts | Instructor: Frank Anselmo | Students: Hongjoon Jang & Haehyun Park | Collaborators: Hongjoon Jang & Haehyun Park

154 PETA FISH Fishing Gun Logo | School: School of Ciusal Arts | Instructor: Frank Anselmo | Students: Camilo Galofre & Tal Midyan | Collaborators: Camilo Galofre & Tal Midyan

154 PETA HORSE Bleeding Bar Code LOGO | School: School of Ciusal Arts | Instructor: Frank Anselmo | Students: Mytran Dang, Gary X Lee & Jin Young Yoo | Collaborators: Camilo Galofre & Tal Midyan | Collaborators: Mytran Dang, Gary X Lee & Jin Young Yoo

155 PETA HORSE Horse Stop Sign LOGO | School: School of Ciusal Arts | Instructor: Frank Anselmo | Students: Hongjoon Jang, Haehyun Park & Min Young Chung | Collaborators: Hongjoon Jang, Haehyun Park & Min Young Chung

156 PETA FISH Ying Yang LOGO | School: School of Ciusal Arts | Instructor: Frank Anselmo | Students: Aksana Berdnikova, Juan Pablo Gomez, Anna Fine & Lindsey Reay | Collaborators: Aksana Berdnikova, Juan Pablo Gomez, Anna Fine & Lindsey Reay

156 PETA FISH Fish Audio LOGO | School: School of Ciusal Arts | Instructor: Frank Anselmo | Students: Duri Lim & Jarwon Jamie Shin | Collaborators: Duri Lim & Jarwon Jamie Shin

156 PETA - The Saving Hand | School: School of Ciusal Arts | Instructor: Frank Anselmo | Students: You Min Woo, Seokmin Hong, Yong Jun Lee, Sanggun Park | Mock Client(s): PETA Fish

Assignment: Create a logo that supports PETA's mission to sensitize humans to the plight of all animals killed for food.

Approach: Neurobiologists have long recognized that fish are intelligent animals capable of feeling the same pain as cats and dogs do. Fish have a nervous system that comprehends and responds to pain as well. When they are pulled out of the water, they undergo excruciating decompression. But there are no established regulations that ensure the humane treatment of fish. Fish have been treated harshly by humans hands. We focused on the concept of liberating fish from human induced pain. In the logo, a fish is being released from a human hand. The hand also signifies a wave, or a body of water, that represents the natural environment where fish ought to be. Through such initiatives of setting the fish free, humans can function both as liberator and a safe haven of living water for fish to thrive.

156 PETA FISH Stop Fishing LOGO | School: School of Ciusal Arts | Instructor: Frank Anselmo | Students: Aksana Berdnikova & Juan Pablo Gomez | Collaborators: Aksana Berdnikova & Juan Pablo Gomez

158 Trailer Cakes Logo | School: Texas A&M University- Commerce | Instructor: Josh Ege | Student: Amanda Crumley | Mock Client(s): Trailer Cakes

158 Bridging The Gap | School: School of Visual Arts | Instructor: Nicolaus Taylor | Student: Jamie Connell

I analyzed what The Gap stands for today and what it could stand for in the future to make it a more successful brand. I came up with the idea of homegrown, gritty, American craft. All denim is personally designed and hand-made by real artisans.

158 Tranquilitea | School: School of Visual Arts | Instructor: Alice Drueding | Student: Carol Ly

Assignment: The goal of this assignment was to create a unique identity for a tea company, setting it apart from other brands through a strong thematic and visual concept. The project included naming the brand as well as developing all of the design components, starting with the logo.

Approach: After coming up with the name "Tranquilitea," I merged a universally familiar symbol from Eastern philosophy with an immediately recognizable reference to tea. The elegant economy of the mark reflects the balance of yin and yang and the essence of tranquility.

158 Tranquilitea | School: School of Visual Arts | Instructor: Alice Drueding | Student: Carol Ly

Assignment: The goal of this assignment was to create a unique identity for a tea company, setting it apart from other brands through a strong thematic and visual concept. The project included naming the brand as well as developing all of the design components, starting with the logo.

Approach: After coming up with the name "Tranquilitea," I merged a universally familiar symbol from Eastern philosophy with an immediately recognizable reference to tea. The elegant economy of the mark reflects the balance of yin and yang and the essence of tranquility.

159 School: School of Visual Arts | Instructor: Alice Drueding | Student: Carol Ly

159 Publican One Color | School: School of Visual Arts | Instructor: Eric Baker | Student: Daniel Rodriguez | Ad Client: Porter Four Pack

160 Boston Opera House Branding | School: School of Visual Arts | Instructor: Adrian Pulfer | Student: TJ Derrick | Mock Client(s): Boston Opera House

Assignment: The Boston Opera House is a theatre with a rich history. Starting as the B. F. Keith Memorial theatre, it was a jewel of it's time for vaudeville production and theatre, and it was built with a sense of luxury that is unrivalled. I wanted to elevate the brand to reflect this rich heritage and beautiful architecture. My goal was, through typography and illustration, to make something elegant and representative of the structure itself. I also wanted to be able to represent the diversity of the theatre and the range of shows and concerts that have played within.

Approach: I first did a brand audit of the Boston Opera House. I observed how they were being represented online and in printed materials. I then looked at the theatre's history and what visual elements could be included in the mark. I found that the structure is very ornate and full of filigree. So I decided to have the primary mark reflect this part of the architecture. I then coupled the illustration with the typeface Didot because of it's elegance and modern appeal. I wanted the mark to be adaptive to the events going on at the theatre so, for a limited amount of larger productions, the center image is able to change. This adaptability emphasizes the diversity of the shows that play at the Opera House and it also gives the customer, through printed materials, a memento of the specific event that they attended.

161 Amanda's Restaurant Menu Redesign | School: School of Visual Arts | Instructor: Gail Anderson | Students: Jonas Christiansen & Rebecca Lim | Typeface Design: Rebecca Lim | Illustrations: Jonas Christiansen | Ad Client: Amanda Cohen | Collaborator: Rebecca Lim

Redesigning the menu of Amanda Cohen's restaurant.

162 Rubin Museum of Art | Student: Pedro Dos Santos | Ad Client: Rubin Museum of Art | School: School of Visual Arts | Instructor(s): Claudia De Almeida and Carin Goldberg

162 MoMA Exhibition Identity for On Line: Drawing Through the Twentieth Century | Student: Minsun Kim | Client: MoMA | Instructor(s): Brigitta Bungard and Julia Hoffmann

166 Museum of Comic and Cartoon Art | Student: Ji Soo Lee | Client: Museum of Comic and Cartoon | School: School of Visual Arts | Instructor(s): Claudia De Almeida, Carin Goldber

168 Museum of the City of New York | School: Brigham Young University | Instructor: Adrian Pulfer | Designer: Kent Miller | Mock Client(s): Museum of the City of New York

Assignment: The Museum of the City of New York celebrates the city, educating the public about its distinctive character, especially its heritage of diversity, opportunity, and perpetual transformation. Founded in 1923 as a private, nonprofit corporation, the Museum connects the past, present, and future of New York City. It serves the people of New York and visitors from around the world through exhibitions, school and public programs, publications, and collections. The project was to create an entirely new identity for the museum that could be effectively integrated across all forms of communication.

Approach: Through the branding I wanted to communicate ideas such as construction, compactness, density, and grid, since these are all leading factors that have shaped the character of New York .

170 Museum of Moving Image | Student: Ji Min Nam | Ad Client: Museum of Moving Image | School: School of Visual Arts | Instructor(s): Claudia De Almeida and Carin Goldberg

172 American Museum of Natural History | Student: Andrew Teoh | Client: American Museum of Natural History | School: School of Visual Arts | Instructor(s): Claudia De Almeida & Carin Goldberg

174 PLATINUM Platinum El Museo Del Barrio | Student: Daniel Rodriguez | Ad Client: El Museo Del Barrio | School: School of Visual Arts | Instructor(s): Claudia De Almeida & Carin Goldberg

176 Dark Nature | School: Ringling College of Art & Design | Instructor: Allen Harrison & Douglas Higgins | Designer: Fernando Rosales & Paul Gonzalez

Approach: Dark Nature entails the feeling of the mysterious and unknown world of the Nocturnal. The concept is "Concealing & Revealing." The concept shows hints but never the whole picture. This concept is derived from trying to see in the dark. The show is broken down into 3 chapters: The Forest, The Cave, and The Ocean. All three are meant to evoke a dangerous and evocative tone. The motion graphic shorts are meant to convey the essence of the places one is to visit. In the poster executions, the animals are featured and the environments hinted at. The type is free flowing through space, and changeable, much like a creature of the night. The sense is one of mystery, curiosity and danger. We feel that passersby with an interest will be immediately drawn in.

178 Neue National Galerie Corporate Rebranding | School: Savannah College of Art and Design | Instructor: Peter Wong | Designer: Aaron Brown | Client(s): Neue National Galerie

Assignment: This project entailed a comprehensive rebranding of Berlin's modern art museum, the Neue Nationalgalerie. Whereas the museum's evocative, minimal architecture makes a bold statement, the Neue Natinalgalerie lacks an equally distinctive brand. Therefore, the primary goal of the rebranding was to develop a logo that draws inspiration from the museum's aesthetic focus on Modernism and its iconic architecture.

Approach: My approach to this project comprised three phases: research, ideation, and production. The research phase primarily focused on distilling the museum's identity, mission statement, and curatorial trends into a small set of essential characteristics. This list of critical adjectives was then abstracted into a short phrase—"N-Squared"— which served as the primary structural metaphor for the remaining phases of design. The ideation phase consisted of developing a logomark and visual vocabulary that embodied the rebranding's primary structural metaphor. The phrase "N-squared" called to mind the repetition of the letter "N" in the museum's name, the repetitious, geometric aesthetic of Mies van der Rohe's architecture, and most pointedly, the shape of a square. These ideas were worked through in visual form via a large number of low-fidelity sketches. The best of these sketches were refined in digital form until a clear front-runner was identified. Once the logomark was complete, it set the stage for developing a complementary visual vocabulary comprising a grid-system that is applicable across a varied collateral and a color palette that derives its colors from Germany's national flag.The production stage of the project involved leveraging the visual vocabulary to design a representative suite of deliverables, including stationery, membership cards, exhibit guides, posters, and a tote bag.

Results: Because this initiative was a student project, the Neue Nationalgalerie was unaware of its development and therefore had no reaction. However, the project was received well. It was awarded gold in the Savannah College of Art and Design's graphic design annual and HOW magazine chose the project for an International Design Award.

180 Daft Punk | Student: Jonas Christiansen | School: School of Visual Srts | Instructor(s): Yego Moravia & Albert Ignacio

Assignment: Daft Punk 7" Cover. The Cover Artwork is created by 144 lines representing each repetition of the line around the world in the song. The Inside shows 5 elements who represent the 5 elements the song is created by. These elements are inspired by the Daft Punk's helmets and spell the word "World". The cover reveals its multiple layers in steps, making it an experience for the customer while listening to the song.

181 Ella Fitzgerald Sings the Best of the Songbooks | School: Tyler School of Art, Temple University | Instructor: Kelly Holohan | Designer: Lydia Nichols

Assignment: This project was executed in the Graduate Thesis course at Tyler School of Art. The prompt for this assignment was "Quiet/Stillness."

182 Escudo De Armas | School: Ringling College of Art & Design | Instructor: Allen Harrison | Designer: Raji Purcell

Approach: ESCUDO DE ARMAS (Coat Of Arms) is a branding project for a fictitious psychedelic flamenco-tronic rock band from Austin Texas. The band consists of two respected musicians from their genres, that have quit to join forces.

184 Drawer-Handles Chess | School: School of Visual Arts | Instructor: Kevin O'Callaghan | Designer: JeongWoo Kim
Assignment: Created object ideas for chess design.
Approach: My creative ideas are between drawer, handles, and chess.

185 Tidal 1, Tidal 2 | School: Savannah College of Art and Design | Instructor: Rhonda Arntsen | Designer: Carlos Báez
Assignment: A visual experiment based on the principles of information design and borrowing from the aesthetic of navigational charts, the tidal series explores the tidal region off the southern coast of Tybee Island, GA. As an area where many drown and rescues happen, the numbers, which would traditionally represent depth in a navigational chart, refer to a legend which employs statistically relevant information (depth, incidents of drowning, number of yearly rescues, height of tides, etc). By mixing the photographic narrative with the statistical information and separating the legend from the images, a multi-layered complexity is achieved, forcing the viewer to engage intently to understand the dangers posed by the tidal region.
Approach: Fascinated by the other-worldly landscape of the tidal regions and the danger the area poses, I knew the project's success would hinge on great photography. After a couple of successful shoots, I knew I had the photographic narratives, but struggled to tie the images to information design. In researching the area, I became interested in the idea of navigational charts and their history in providing safe passage for ship captains trying to navigate unfamiliar waters. It seemed natural to rely on the structure and context (safety) of the navigational chart as an overlay and use the numbers to call out statistically relevant information a Tybee Island local should know.

187 Interactive AQI Bike | School: Rhode Island School of Design | Instructor: Kelly Dobson | Designer: Kyuha Shim | Client(s): Department of Environmental Management RI
Assignment: This project explores sensible communications by visualizing the quality of outdoor air in our surrounding environment. I sought to create responsive narratives between a bicycle rider and audiences. For effective communication, I made a system displaying four different text messages based on the level of Carbon Monoxide.
Approach: As an interaction designer, the process of creating circular matrices for my bike was a big challenge. I visited the Nature Lab at Rhode Island School of Design to observe natural objects that have circular geometries. Inspired by those objects, I developed the circular rasterizing system to translate my text messages into rotating binary grids on my bike-wheel. Then, I hacked the custom light-emitting device and made the visual systems responsive to the air quality of the user's surroundings. This way, we can capture the detailed information of air quality in real-time.
Results: This project enabled me to further my multi-disciplinary practices. I believe that the Interactive Bike will enhance human perception of space and expand the spectrum of informative communication.

188 Stella Food Packaging | Student Name: Lynne Yun | Ad Client: Stella | School: School of Visual Arts | Instructor(s): Louise Fili
Assignment: Greek textile patterns and greek symbols were combined to create a high-end product packaging.

189 La Sera Packaging | Student: Lynne Yun | Ad Client: La Sera | Instructor(s): Louise Fili

190 The Three Little Pigs | Student Name: Daniel Rodriguez | School: School of Visual Arts | Instructor(s): Claudia De Almeida & Carin Goldberg
192 Kepler Orbital Space Travel Packaging | School: Drexel University, Antoinette Westphal College of Media Arts & Design | Instructor: Jody Graff | Designer: Nicholas Lim
Assignment: For my senior thesis project, I designed a Kepler Orbital Space Travel Package. Kepler Orbital Space Travel's name and logo are inspired by the astronomer Johannes Kepler. The kit is designed for the company's clients.
Approach: The system (kit) uses the color gradients and progressions to lead users deeper into their journey, as they move from the lighter blues and tan of earth and its atmosphere into the dark hues of space.

194 Omiki Sake | School: California State University, Fullerton | Instructor: Theron Moore | Designer: Khoa Nguyen | Client(s): Omiki Sake
Assignment: The assignment is to create an unique high-end sake packaging, which is totally different from normal sake bottles we usually see on market.
Approach: To bring a different take on this packaging, I dive into rich Japanese traditional culture. I use sake flasks as the bottles and dress them up with traditional clothing (samurai and geisha kimono). To emphasis more on the Japanese culture, I use Japanese fabric to wrap around the canister and the bottle. Each canis-

ter also contains a pouch, which is carefully wrapped around the canister label, as an surprise option to carry the bottle.
Results: The result is an interesting packaging with rich cultural references that you don't see normally on the market.

195 Wine Packaging | School: Penn State University | Instructor: Kristin Breslin Sommese | Designer: Demi Ngai

196 Wine Packaging | School: Penn State University | Instructor: Kristin Breslin Sommese | Designer: Sierra Finn

197 *Assignment:* Bath and Body Product Line | School: Penn State University | Instructor: Kristin Breslin Sommese | Designer: Cecile Jordan
Assignment: A bath and body product line for dogs

198 TANKED Brewery | School: California State University, Fullerton | Instructor: Theron Moore | Designer: Tyler Ruffino | Mock Client(s): TANKED Brewery
Assignment: The project was to come up with a concept and create a prototype package for a fictitious beverage. Any beverage could be used and how much we wanted to develop the concept was up to the student so long as the final product showed evidence of a cohesive idea. The name of the beverage as well as any company associated with the beverage was entirely up to the student to create.
Approach: Considering the fact that I was designing for a company named "Tanked," I immediately made connections to military tanks. The idea of a crate style box with tank shell bottles came early on, but the look of both was vastly different in early stages of design. The box was, at first, just photographs of wooden crate imposed on cardboard with perforations for opening while the bottles were to simply have labels that looked like brushed copper (with text and such). Upon completion of this initial mock up, I was unhappy with the product and decided to push the idea further. The box was an easy change (aside from fabrication), but the bottles were more difficult of a problem to solve. I re-examined various photos of tank shells and looked into new materials. It was at this point that I decided to really push the look of the bottles by carefully using metallic paint and hand-made stencils to give a more authentic look. To really bring the entire idea together, I fitted the box with hinges and stenciled text as well as packing hay.

199 Udderly Perfect Dairy | School: California State University Fullerton | Instructor: Theron Moore | Designer: Tiffany Libman | Mock Client(s): Udderly Perfect Dairy
Assignment: The assignment was to develop a package design concentrating on liquid packaging. The product could range from water to alcohol (any liquid that is consumable).
Approach: I knew most of the students would choose alcohol, so I chose a product that you use everyday: milk. I wanted to incorporate beautiful typography on a simplistic background; the white of the milk to make the design pop! My inspiration for the typography comes from the CBS cafeteria wall designed by Lou Dorfsman. I had many different versions of the label, first in all color then black and white with additions of color as to not overwhelm the design. I also wanted to make a carrier for the milk bottles that is reminiscent of the door-to-door crates from the thirties and forties, but with a modern twist. I researched everything about the antique milk bottles down to the caps in the top of the bottle which you know today as POGS. To make the packaging look as real as possible without filling it with milk, I painted the inside of the bottles with white acrylic paint.
Results: The results were amazing ad my professor was very proud of the finished product, and so was I.

200 Grizzly Whiskey | School: California State University Fullerton | Instructor: Theron Moore | Designer: Jon Cox | Mock Client(s): Grizzly Whiskey
Assignment: For my beverage/packaging design project I chose to create a straight whiskey based out of the state of California in the United States. The grizzly bear is iconic to California and is even featured on the state flag, so it became the theme of my fictional company, appropriately named Grizzly Whiskey.
Approach: The problem was to make the design scream grizzly bear, without having an actual bear incorporated into the solution. In order to do this, I simplified the form into things that could represent a bear. In the wild, bears mark their territory by slashing trees as high up as they can reach, to demonstrate their size to other bears in the area. The claw marks became the "logo" for the company, which is etched into the bottle itself. Keeping true to the tradition of marking whiskey jugs with X's to show age, each claw mark represents ten years, making this a 40-year old bottle. The name GRIZZLY shows through the bottle and is printed on hand-burned vintage paper. I carved the cork in the image of a bear's tooth, and the packaging became a hollowed-tree log, with wood-burned tree rings as well as the claw mark logo on the back. When the box is opened, the bottle sits on a pedestal with the slogan "Get Grizzly" shining through, complete with a small body of text to read after the bottle is removed.
Results: This project was made for Theron Moore's Special Stud-

ies in Graphic Design class at Cal State Fullerton, and my solution earned an A.

201 The Milk House | School: California State University, Fullerton | Instructor: Theron Moore | Designer: Jamie Yonaki | Mock Client(s): The Milk House

Assignment: The project required creating and designing packaging for any type of drinkable liquid. The project also called for naming the liquid and designing its logo.

Approach: The Whole-Hole concept started out as a linguistic based project looking into lexical and typographic ambiguity. As the research progressed, this developed into the idea of duality and how one concept needs its opposite concept to have meaning and context. Image needs text, movement needs stasis, and black needs white. Using linguistic playfulness and duality, the homophones whole and hole were used to take this concept from the intangible into the tangible via fashion and photography. Neoprene Smoothskin was used to create this garment as it allowed the bodysuit to have dual modes of existence, on land and underwater. The holes were intuitively hand cut with the aim of covering what was necessary without compromising the naked body's visual magnetism.

Results: The client was very much satisfied and was pleased with the approach I took. The client was especially pleased with and appreciated the theme in which I chose to design and create the entire package.

202 Fluxus Poster | School: School of Visual Arts | Instructor: Carin Goldberg | Designer: Yi-Chen"Jessi" Tsai | Mock Client(s): The Museum of Modern Art

Assignment: Design a Poster for "Thing/ Thought Fluxus" show at the Museum of Modern Art in New York City. Thing/ Thought Fluxus Editions, an ambitious publishing program conceived by artist and designer George Maciunas, a central figure in the group, comprises affordable items made in multiples intended to communicate the group's ideas and activities on an international scale.

203 Kcai Theoretical Lecture Poster | School: Kansas City Art Institute | Instructor: Marty Maxwell Lane | Designer: Trent Roach | Mock Client(s): Kansas City Art Institute

Assignment: This project explored typographic and graphic hierarchy though the design of materials announcing a hypothetical design lecture at Kansas City Art Institute. The objectives were to investigate the work and process of a designer to inform and inspire my personal work and create a poster that would visually engage an audience and raise interest for the event.

Approach: The designer investigated was Nigel Holmes, a British graphic designer. Nigel has been a successful freelance designer and illustrator for Time and has opened a personal Illustration company who serves clients such as Apple, Fortune and Nike. He believes that information should be beautiful and often uses a simple approach in illustration with simple coloring to display it. Nigels' love for information inspired an info graphic approach showing the time and place of the event along with the gravity of his success. I took a piece of the Vanderslice Auditorium, a light fixture, and used its circular decoration to further hint at his love for beautiful information

204 Trisha Brown Dance Company | School: School of Visual Arts | Instructor: Carin Goldberg | Designer: You Min Woo | Mock Client(s): Trisha Brown Dance Company at MoMA

Assignment: Design posters for a series of performances by the Trisha Brown Dance Company, at MoMA.

Approach: Trisha Brown Dance Company performances at MoMA show dance in two dimensions, allowing it to be seen in a gallery setting. But if one considers lines as the trace of a point in motion, an idea at the core of this project, the very act of dance becomes a drawing, an insertion of line into time. The TBDC performances at MoMA were called Sticks, Scallops, Locus Solo and Roof Piece Re-Layed. All four performances have a strong relationship to line and reveal the basic relationship between structure and dancer. For each performance, I visualized what the dance would look like as a drawing of lines and dots across a period of time of their performance. In all four posters, lines are drawn imperfectly with a pencil to show the organic movements and the orientation of the dancer's bodies. The dots are perfect solid circles that show the placement of the dancers in space.

205 World of Dreams | School: Penn State University | Instructor: Kristin Breslin Sommese | Designer: Erika Fischerkeller | Other(s): Photographer: Erika Fischerkeller

Assignment: Students developed a poster for the Ann Arbor Film Festival entitled "World of Dreams," in which they designed and photographed surrealistic scenes.

206 Think, Feel, Create, Solve | School: Savannah College of Art and Design | Instructor: Shawn McKinney | Designer: Brian Biles

Assignment: Completed in my Poster Design class, the objective of this project was to design a single poster using illustrative imagery that serves as a vehicle for event marketing/promotion, social-

intervention awareness, or political propaganda. The focus of the poster design was to be determined by its category selection, along with the specific needs of the target audience. We were limited to using three PMS colors and any physical size or orientation.

Approach: I began the project by researching the role that illustration has played throughout the history of poster design as a communication medium and specifically looked at historical as well as contemporary examples. At the same time, I read Tim Brown's book Change By Design and learned about the concept of design thinking. The first step was a comparative analysis of multiple Illustration styles and techniques that were intended to broaden my understanding about the communication potential of illustration as a visual medium. Using the knowledge gained from my research, I then created three exploratory studies focusing on the development of illustrative imagery specific to my research and ideas. These were more experimental in approach, exploring potential directions I wanted to move in. Following this, I developed a concise and extensive creative brief identifying the project overview, specs, goals, deliverables, target audiences, creative tone and image, major questions, people and processes, competition and schedule. Additionally I developed mood boards and compiled visual inspiration specific to the project. I then drafted the poster text as appropriate to the specific needs identified in the creative brief. The next step consisted of developing multiple preliminary thumbnail sketches and comps based off of the creative brief. From these rough thumbnail sketches I moved on to creating two developed digital roughs exploring multiple compositional and color variations for each idea. The final stage consisted of choosing one digital rough for continued refinement. While I was not working directly with a client, throughout the entire process I was presenting each stage of the project, responding to critical feedback and criticism from my instructor and peers and making changes to the design as necessary. The process itself was very collaborative and reflexive and I was constantly being informed from multiple directions.

Results: The final design has been well received thus far by my Professor and peers. It recently garnered a semifinalist placing in the Print Communications category of the 2012 Adobe Design Achievement Awards.

207 Wine Packagingm | School: Penn State University | Instructor: Kristin Breslin Sommese | Designer: Demi Ngai

Assignment: Self-promotional wine packaging

207 World of Dreams | School: Penn State University | Instructor: Kristin Breslin Sommese | Designer: Kimberly Price

Assignment: Students developed a poster for the Ann Arbor Film Festival entitled "World of Dreams," in which they designed and photographed surrealistic scenes.

208 World of Dreams | School: Penn State University | Instructor: Kristin Breslin Sommese | Designer: Darcy Rose

208 World of Dreams | School: Penn State University | Instructor: Kristin Breslin Sommese | Designer: Michael Morris

209 PLATINUM PGP | School: School of Visual Arts | Instructor(s): Peter Ahlberg

212 Joshua Lutz on Walt Whitman | Student: Diane Wilder | Ad Client: The Morgan Library | School: School of Visual Arts | Instructor(s): Peter Ahlberg

Description: A posters series for Joshua Lutz, an American photographer showcasing his beautiful imagery of his hometown, Meadowland, New Jersey. Each poster holds selected verses from The Leaves of Grass (1855) by Walt Whitman.

213 Folly Theater "Vijay Iyer Trio" Jazz Poster | School: Kansas City Art Institute | Instructor: Tyler Galloway | Designer: Zacree Cobos | Mock Client(s): Folly Theater

Assignment: The assignment was to express an artist's music and stage presence.

214 Memento Mori Literary Festival Posters | School: Tyler School of Art, Temple University | Instructor: Kelly Holohan | Designer: Caleb Heisey

Assignment: The poster series was executed in the Graduate Thesis course at Tyler School of Art. The Graphic & Interactive Design MFA program stresses self authorship. The broad theme given on this assignment was "Language".

Approach: The Memento Mori Literary Festival is a series of autumn events which celebrates the theme of death in literature and the legendary authors of the past. The poster series pairs festival events with the untimely deaths of our most beloved writers such as Keats, Poe, and Hemingway. I used collage as a medium to depict the authors in a dark yet quirky way, to both idolize these figures while speaking to the festival's light-hearted nature.

215 Vote | School: California State University Fullerton | Instructor: Theron Moore | Designer: Matthew Nieblas | Mock Client(s): N/A

Assignment: The assignment was to create a "get out the vote" poster. I wanted my poster to challenge the viewer to imagine what life without the power to vote looked like. In essence, my concept was "without the right to vote (or the will to vote) an individual lives in bondage to their government." I hand applied the scars to the model's back and created the word "vote" with hand made scars as well. The model's hands are bound with chain behind his back and the poster is given an overwhelming red tint in order to convey a violent tone.

Approach: I began this project with research. I wanted to really understand the importance of voting and what life looked like for people without the power to vote. I then began to make thumbnails and to research other political/social posters. After choosing my best thumbnails and ideas I made several comps. Then I chose one comp and revised it until it was finished and became the poster you see now.

216 Antwerp Six | School: Art Center College of Design | Instructor: Clive Piercy | Designer: David Badounts | Mock Client(s): London Fashion Week
Assignment: London Fashion Week is an exhibition that takes place twice a year at the Somerset House in Central London, which showcases some of the world's most prominent fashion designers. The Antwerp Six were some of the first attendees of the show in the early eighties. Antwerp Six is an influential Belgian avant-garde collective of fashion designers who have made an immeasurable impact on the fashion world since the 1980s with radical and distinct garment and fabric forms. The group consists of Walter Van Beirendonck, Ann Demeulemeester, Dries van Noten, Dirk Van Saene, Dirk Bikkembergs and Marina Yee. The identity consists of six 22 x 33" posters, a foldable catalog, invitations, calendar, as well as moving environmental stage design elements projected onto fabric and stucco covered walls.

Approach: The designers, influenced by their Belgian roots, succumbed to research into Flemish and Baroque master painters and sculptors, including Jan van Eyck, Paul Rubens, Alexander Adriaenssen, and Rogier van der Weyden. To create a system for the Antwerp Six, central thematic elements had to be created in order create a derivative framework for the six artists, which are radically different, but from similar roots. Each poster with the aforementioned designers take fabric used from the runway through the same fabric, garment and textile explorations as processed by the designers themselves.

Results: The result was presented in an exhibition type show, suspended posters, with documentations of how the stage elements would be presented via a projector behind the larger poster series. The catalogues, invitations and real world scenarios were also presented in order to showcase how it functions in actual locations such as the London Underground, buildings in East London district of Shoreditch and other places which have a climate for fashion enthusiasts.

218 Inspired By Music | School: Penn State University | Instructor: Lanny Sommese | Designer: Sarah Dewlin Other(s): Illustrator: Sarah Dewlin
Assignment: Design a poster for a student competition with the theme "Inspired By Music."

219 Modernism: A Design Retrospective | School: Coastal Carolina University | Instructor: Scott Mann | Designer: Marcello Garofalo | Mock Client(s): Museum of Modern Art
Assignment: Create a poster for an exhibition and lecture series being held at the Museum of Modern Art titled "Modernism: A Design Retrospective." The content should reflect the spirit of the Modernist movement from multiple perspectives: literature, art, cinema, poetry, etc.
Approach: My design is inspired by Filippo Tommaso Marinetti. Modernists reveled in simplicity in form and simplification of ideas, therefore the windows are primary colors near the top. The positioning reflects change from the emphasis on realism, which was associated with fine art and canons of the Renaissance, to more accessible and easily understood art form based on geometric shapes and bold use of color. The street side perspective looking up the building's facade alludes to the exhibition as a retrospective and the centered type keeps the composition moving inward while accentuating the colored windows proximity to the left.

220 Origami Convention | Student: Minjung Suh | Ad Client: Origami Convention | School: School of Visual Arts | Instructor(s): Nicolaus Taylor
Description: This is a project to create the brand identity for the event: Origami Convention.

222 XIT | School: Ringling College of Art & Design | Instructor: Edwin Utermohlen | Designer: Heather Burrell
Approach: XIT [eg-sit, ek-sit] Wine and Grill is a restaurant that fuses both the food and cultures of California cuisine with Texas barbecue. The restaurant is located in Los Angeles and XIT is a historical ranch in Texas. The iconography comes from the ranch's branding marks. XIT Wine and Grill is known for selling their bar-

becue sauce and wine bottles, all in their own unique packaging.

224 Grow Gardening Shopping Bag | School: California State University Fullerton | Instructor: Theron Moore | Designer: Matthew Nieblas
Assignment: The goal of this project was to create a shopping bag for the store of our choosing. I chose a fictional boutique gardening shop named Grow Gardening. I wanted my bag to visually indicate the benefits of shopping at Grow Gardening (while being conceptually and visually intriguing). The benefit of shopping at Grow Gardening is (as the bag indicates) that what you purchase there will nurture and cause your plants to grow. The bag appears as a cross section of soil with a root system and a small sprout rising above the "ground" plane of the bag. Pulling up on the sprout causes the plant to "grow" (the plant is folded and rests in a loose pocket which allows the plant to unfold and "grow"). As the plant is pulled upward a panel slides into place completing the root system and cryptically spelling the word "grow." The plant is then folded over and several of its leaves slide into pockets, allowing the plant to be used as a handle.

Approach: I knew from the start that I wanted to capitalize on the interactive nature of the handle. I spent hours creating thumbnails and trying to resolve how best to use the handle. My idea underwent many revisions in order to make it a practical solution that also stayed as true as possible to my concept. I wanted the bag to be photographic in order to enhance the "realism" of the plant growing. Additionally the photographic nature of a bag made of dirt is rather striking visually. I created the root system by collecting the branches of ground covering (apple ice plant) and arranging them with floral wire. I created the typography "grow" the same way. The cross section of dirt was created with potting soil and a picture of dirt/rock. I collected vines for the plant and then photographed all the individual elements. I created the bag multiple times in order to refine the way in which the sprout "grows" and how the panel which completes the roots slides into place. The end result allows a seamless transition from sprout to fully grown plant and root system to functional handle.

Results: I received an "A" on this project and a positive critique based upon my dedication to an unique concept and striking execution.

226 PLATINUM Castro 1959 | School: The Art Institute of Houston | Instructor: Michele Damato | Designer: Melissa Cadavid
Assignment: The design of Castro 1959 began by an assignment given by Professor Michele Damato in a typography expressive class. The concept of the assignment is to create an alphabet based off of anything creative. A major part of the project was the creation of a good concept. The goal is not only to create an out of the ordinary and interesting alphabet but also to create a concept that stands by the design which makes the alphabet one united strong design.

Approach: The alphabet Castro 1959 began from an article that I read about religious oppression in Cuba. The article stated that a communist party from a department of religious matters violently assaulted a home of a woman who is a devout catholic. The communist party took any religious item this woman had and destroyed them, leaving this woman with no intact religious items in her own home. After reading this article I began to elaborate a design where I can illustrate what was left of the religious assault in that woman's home. I used many typical catholic items such as rosaries, crosses, figurines of the Virgin Mary, prayers candles, the Cuban flag, and other things as such. I took each Item and purposely broke them down into pieces to represent the assault against the woman, after taking each item and destroying them I burned some of them to represent how her freedom of religion was burned down. The Cuban flag was used to show how religion is mistreated in a country where the Catholic religion is a major part of the culture. All together I used the destroyed items and began to design every single letter of the Spanish alphabet. The name Castro 1959 was chosen by me because of the relation of the religious oppression in Cuba. In 1959 the Cuban Revolution began and right after Fidel Castro became president of Cuba. After the communist revolution, Cuba restricted religious practices which led to many persecutions, until this day even though religious freedom is now accepted as long as it respects the law, things such as the article I read, keep occurring I Cuba. All together this concept, design and facts represents the typographic alphabet of Castro 1959.
Results: The client, being my professor, admired my dedication and hard work to achieve what I accomplished. Ms.Damato evaluated my alphabet and was a major part of every single improvement I would make in this piece.

228 Chimera | Student: Britta Carlson | School: School Of Visual Arts | Instructor(s): Yaeger Moravia St Victor

*Description: Chimera is a typeface I illustrated where each letter is comprised of two animals. The heads of the animals start with the same letter as they are representing, for example the "bat fish" assumes the role of the B and the "panda chicken" for the P. All letters were hand drawn by me.

229 Garçonic Typeface | School: York University / Sheridan College Joint Program in Design | Instructor: E.A. (Zab) Hobart | Designer: Yosub Jack Choi

Assignment: I studied typography for three years and learned about basics and fundamentals of typography. In my third year, I took a course called "typeface design" and spent the whole semester working on my first typeface called Garçonic. The challenge was to design a typeface that is simple, legible and unique. Garçonic is a modern display typeface that combines unique characteristics from Egyptian slab serif and San-serif typefaces. The typeface consists of uppercase, lowercase letters and numbers.

Approach: The major intention of the project was to bring something that is historical and add modern characteristics to make something, which is highly contemporary yet still, reflects the past. In the 1800s, the slab serif typefaces, also known as Egyptian typeface, were very popular especially when typewriters were widely used. Sans-serif typefaces also have a long history, however, they were very popular and used mostly in the 1900s and the 2000s. I wanted to capture different movements, cultures and styles of the two periods.

Results: The typeface is very unique but it is very legible and does not hold any specific image or message, and therefore it has a lot of potential to be used broadly. The typeface can be applied in many different ways including, but not limited to, magazines, a variety of advertisements and commercials, logos, and graphics for packaging designs. I designed two posters and business cards to showcase and promote the typeface. I continued the same ideas and intentions and carried the same visual aesthetics.

230 AIGA Type | School: Kansas State University | Instructor: Dan Warner | Designer: Jason Wright | Mock Client(s): AIGA (Kansas State University)

Assignment: This project was to create a unique logotype for promotion of the local AIGA chapter that would reflect the forward-thinking nature of the organization and stir up interest on campus and in the community.

Approach: With this mark, I didn't want to funnel myself into one specific style or trend as to reflect the assortment of visual directions that are used by the contemporary designer. Instead, I wanted to create a truly original mark combining traditional, capital letterforms, and the modern simplicity of lowercase forms. I researched classic calligraphy and hand lettering to gather elements for the uppercase structure and the flourishes that would create the simple lowercase framework.

Results: The result is a distinctive logotype that nods at traditional influences on design and looks forward to modern graphic design ideas with which the chapter was very pleased. The logotype is being used on the organization's print materials, t-shirts, and website throughout the 2012-2013 school year with favorable response from the community.

231 Crease Typeface | School: The Art Institute of Houston | Instructor: Michelle Damato | Designer: Amilia Ramirez

Assignment: The project was to develop an experimental typeface while utilizing other than traditional means. Items and found objects surrounding strong concepts were encouraged as opposed to developing a traditional font digitally. In addition to the criteria, I also applied a personal challenge by preferring my execution to utilize an element that was fairly difficult, or impossible, to maneuver or control in addition to a tangible medium.

Approach: My concept surrounded the philosophical impact each individual creates through merely existing. Similar to the butterfly and ripple effects, an action done may have an indirect impact on the futures of loved ones and strangers. To show this, the tangible medium I used was textured paper while the uncontrolled elements I used were light and shadow. I scored creases in simple squares of paper that would be exposed to morning light to create a single letter. I tried to keep the lines created to a minimum, as I wanted the shadows to be emphasized the most. The shadows covered the descending portion of the creased paper, which beautifully portrayed the wave of impact a single individual, or crease, has on existence. Unintentional, yet unavoidable, smaller creases within individual letters surprisingly express the concept even more so. With the paper being so delicate, it would be impossible to return it to it's original, crisp state once touched. This furthers my expression of individual impact as these smaller creases appeared while the letters were in development. Finally to show all of this clearly and beautifully, I've made the typeface monochromatic to better show the light and shadows. Each letter was carefully crafted to hold a

particular shape and each holds a different intensity of shadow—such as each individual holds and offers a different impact.

Results: This project was for a Typography Expressive class. The result of my typeface was an 'A' for the project, the process, and for the class.

234 Douglas Stratton - Architecture | School: Art Institute of Atlanta | Instructor: Phil Bekker | Designer: Douglas Stratton

Assignment: An architectural study with movement and strong design for a Location 1 assignment.

235 Delano Jones - Tungsten Portrait | School: Art Institute of Atlanta | Instructor: Phil Bekker | Designer: Delano Jones

Assignment: A portrait assignment using Tungsten focusing spot lighting, to incorporate strong shadows

236 Whole-Hole | School: Whanganui School of Design (Universal College of Education) | Instructor: Jo Giddens | Designer: Stefanie McKnight | Other(s): Model: Luca Bartlett

Assignment: The goal of this assignment was to research, analyze and synthesise a chosen concept. This conceptual investigation was then to be developed from an intellectual idea into the design for a product or service.

Approach: The Whole-Hole concept started out as a linguistic based project looking into lexical and typographic ambiguity. As the research progressed, this developed into the idea of duality and how one concept needs its opposite concept to have meaning and context. Image needs text, movement needs stasis, and black needs white.

237 PLATINUM Chad Kelley - Shoes | School: Art Institute of Atlanta | Instructor: Phil Bekker | Designer: Chad Kelley

Assignment: Shoe assignment for "Trends in Contemporary Photography" course.

238 Bobbi Dunn - Shoes | School: Art Institute of Atlanta | Instructor: Phil Bekker | Designer: Bobbi Dunn

Approach: A contemporary and surreal approach to shoe shopping, reminicient of Black Friday.

239 Wheelchair | School: The Art Institute of Atlanta | Instructor: Bekker, Phil | Student: McDonald, John | Client: Art Institute of Atlanta

240 Transition | School: The Art Institute of Houston | Instructor: David Bennet | Designer: Melissa Cadavid

Assignment: The photograph Transition began by an assignment given by Professor David Bennet. The assignment was to find a designer you know and capture a photograph of them in the most out of the ordinary style. The designer was to show you their work and describe to you about their style of work and what made them choose design as their career. Once you know the designer well enough, you can capture them in a situation contrary to their type of design and style. The goal of the assignment was to have an element of surprise that shocked the viewer as soon as it was viewed.

Approach: The idea to photograph Transition initiated from the diversity of the model's design. I choose Graphic designer Brandi Hernandez whose designs are very typographical. As a designer, Hernandez is very organized and likes to maintain a sense of stability in her work. While she constantly intents to have perfect hierarchy and use of leading and kerning, I took that knowledge and began visually illustrating a way to manipulate that sense of perfectness. Before becoming a designer, Hernandez was a dancer, knowing that I illustrated the transition from dancer to graphic designer in this photograph. While wearing a leotard, Hernandez laid on a railroad track to represent the road she is going on. The white powder represents the base of construction of a new life while it also hides the era that ended. While some rocks are covered in powder, the ones going through her chest and up her stomach, which are not covered in powder, represents the past she is now taking to become a graphic designer. The rocks that are covered represents the era that ended in her life and that is left behind as a structure of learning and knowledge. While this photograph is all about change, growth and balance, the word Transition seemed to fit perfectly because of the representation of her life in this abstracted way.

241 Red Baron | School: Art Institute of Atlanta | Instructor: Phil Bekker | Designer: Melissa Pierschbacher

Assignment: Part of my 'Specialization' portfolio on Digital Illustration, where I illustrated people in historic or cinematic events.

242 Lamp | School: Art Institute of Atlanta | Instructor: Phil Bekker | Designer: Bobbi Dunn

Assignment: Location 2 assignment of a lit lamp in a location, where Zone techniques are employed to achieve specific tonal values in the product and location.

Approach: A monochromatic approach using a contrast between product and surroundings.

SchoolDirectory

Art Center College of Design www.artcenter.edu
Hillside Campus: 1700 Lida Street, Pasadena, CA 91103, United States
South Campus: 950 South Raymond Avenue, Pasadena, CA 91105, United States
Tel 626 396 2200

The Art Institute of Atlanta www.artinstitutes.edu/atlanta
6600 Peachtree Dunwoody Road, Atlanta, GA 30328-1649, United States
Tel 770 394 8300 / 1 800 275 4242 | Fax 770 394 0008

The Art Institute of Houston www.artinstitutes.edu/houston
1900 Yorktown, Houston, TX 77056, United States
Tel 713 623 2040 / 1 800 275 4244 | Fax 713 966 2797

Brigham Young University www.byu.edu
150 East 1230 North, Provo, UT 84602, United States
Tel 801 422 4636

California State University - Fullerton www.fullerton.edu
800 North State College Boulevard, Fullerton, CA 92831-3599, United States
Tel 404-679-4500

Coastal Carolina University www.coastal.edu
1866 Southern Lane, Decatur, GA 30033-4097, United States
Tel 972 548 6790

Drexel University, Antoinette Westphal College of Media Arts & Design
www.drexel.edu/westphal
Nesbitt Hall, 33rd and Market Streets, Philadelphia, PA 19104, United States
Tel 215 895 1834

George Brown College www.georgebrown.ca
PO Box 1015, Station B, Toronto, Ontario, M5T 2T9, Canada
Tel 1 800 265 2002

Kansas City Art Institute www.kcai.edu
4415 Warwick Blvd. Kansas City, MO 64111 800-522-5224
Tel 816-472-4852

Kansas State University http://www.k-state.edu
Manhattan, KS 66506
Tel 785-532-6011

Miami Ad School, San Francisco www.miamiadschool.com
415 Jackson Street, Suite B, San Francisco, California 94111, United States
Tel 415 837 0966

Penn State University www.psu.edu
201 Shields Building, Box 3000, University Park, PA 16804, United States
Tel 814 865 5471 | Fax 814 863 7590

Pratt Institute www.pratt.edu
200 Willoughby Avenue, Brooklyn, NY 11205, United States
Tel 718 636 3600 | Fax 718 636 3670

Rhode Island School of Design www.risd.edu
Two College Street
Providence, RI 02903-2784 USA
Tel 401 454-6100

Ringling College of Art & Design www.ringling.edu
2700 North Tamiami Trail
Sarasota, FL 34234-5895
Tel 941-351-5100

Savannah College of Art & Design www.scad.edu
1600 Peachtree Street, NE, Atlanta, GA 30309, United States
Tel 877 722 3285 / 404 253 2700

School of Visual Arts www.schoolofvisualarts.edu
209 East 23rd Street, New York, NY 10010, United States
Tel 212 593 2000 | Fax 212 725 3587

Texas A&M University - Commerce www.web.tamu-commerce.edu
2600 South Neal Street, Commerce, TX 75428, United States
Tel 903 886 5102

Tyler School of Art, Temple University www.temple.edu/tyler
7725 Penrose Avenue, Elkins Park, PA 19027, United States
Tel 215 782 2875

Whanganui School of Design www.wsd.ac.nz
16 Rutland St, Whanganui, N.Z
Tel + 64 6 965 3801

York University www.yorku.ca
4700 Keele Street, Toronto, Ontario, M3J 1P3, Canada
Tel 416 736 2100

Award-Winning Schools

Award-Winning Instructors

Award-Winning Students

GraphisTitles:

Poster Annual 2013

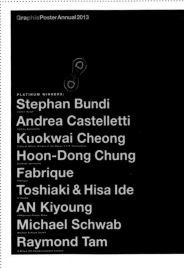

2013
Hardcover: 240 pages
200-plus color illustrations
Trim: 8.5 x 11.75"
ISBN: 1-931241-29-8
US $120

Graphis Poster 2013 is the definitive showcase of the 100 best Posters of the year chosen from numerous international entries. The collection features 9 Platinum and 91 Gold award-winning Posters from Italy, South Africa, Switzerland, Korea, The Netherlands, Japan and the United States, amongst many others. Graphis also features an interview with **Rick Valicenti**, the founder and Design Director of Thirst in Chicago — a firm devoted to "art, function and real human presence."

Advertising Annual 2013

2013
Hardcover: 256 pages
200-plus color images
Trim: 7 x 11 3/4"
ISBN: 1-932026-79-5
US $120

Graphis Advertising 2013 presents some of the top campaigns of the year selected from hundreds of entries. Featured are seasoned works from accomplished advertising agencies, such as **Goodby, Silverstein & Partners, Bailey Lauerman, BVK, DeVito/Verdi, HOOK,** and **Saatchi & Saatchi.** Each spread presents the work with a case study description written by each agency. These campaigns provide insight into the agency's creative process and how they met the needs of their clients.

Design Annual 2013

2013
Hardcover: 256 pages
200-plus color images
Trim: 8.5 x 11.75"
ISBN: 1-932026-77-1
US $120

Graphis Design 2013 features the most compelling design work of the year selected from hundreds of international entries. This volume includes Platinum award – winning entries from **Alt Group, GQ Magazine, Turner Duckworth, Strømme Throndsen Design** and **White Studio.** All published entries are presented on a spread with a case study description written by each designer or design firm.

Branding 6

2013
Hardcover: 256 pages
200-plus color images
Trim: 8.5 x 11.75"
ISBN: 1-932026-78-8
US $120

This book presents interviews, company profiles and visual histories of some of the biggest names in design and retail today, including: Q&A with **Pentagram, WAX, People design, Cue, Firewood, The General Design Co., Studio International,** and **Alt Group.** All that, plus hundreds of images from the year's Graphis Gold Award-winning branding campaigns. This is a must-have for anyone interested in successful, creative branding – designers, businesses, students and fans alike.

Photography Annual 2013

2013
Hardcover: 256 pages
200-plus color images
Trim: 8.5 x 11.75"
ISBN: 1-931241-80-1
US $120

Photography2013 is a moving collection of the years best photographs. Shot by some of the world's most respected photographers and selected from an international pool of entries, these beautifully reproduced images are organized by category for easy referencing. This year's book includes an interview with photographer **Bill Diadato**, discussing his background and the inspiration behind his work.

Masters of the 20th Century

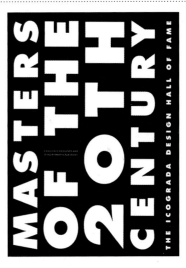

2012
Hardcover: 360 pages
200-plus color illustrations
Trim: 10 x 12"
ISBN: 1-888001-85-2
US $70

This is a huge volume that features the work and biographies of more than 100 top designers worldwide. Designed and edited by **Mervyn Kurlansky**, with distinct profiles of **Pierre Bernard, Wolfgang Weingart** and many others. A testament to exceptional talents and proof that they'll be remembered for generations to come, this book comes complete with a companion CD-ROM containing hundreds of additional images. Forewards by **Steven Heller** and **Marion Wesel-Henrion.**